Don't State It...
Communicate It!

How to Put Clout
In Your
Letters,
Memos,
Reports,
and Proposals

by Robert M. Hochheiser

BARRON'S EDUCATIONAL SERIES, INC.
Woodbury, New York • London • Toronto • Sydney

All inquiries should be addressed to:

Barron's Educational Series, Inc.
113 Crossways Park Drive
Woodbury, NY 11797

International Standard Book No. 0–8120–2650–0

Library of Congress Cataloging No. 84–24309

Library of Congress Cataloging in Publication Data

Hochheiser, Robert M., 1938 –
Don't state it—communicate it!

Bibliography: p. 178
Includes index.
1. Commercial correspondence. 2. Business report writing. I. Title.
HF5721.H57 1985   808'.066651   84–24309
ISBN 0–8120–2650–0

PRINTED IN THE UNITED STATES OF AMERICA
56789 800 987654321

CONTENTS

To
Harry and David

PREFACE

We're in bad shape when we are unable to differentiate between our objectives and the means necessary to meet those objectives. The knowledge and skills necessary to manufacture a good football, for example, are not the same as those necessary to score a touchdown. Similarly, being able to forge a hammer doesn't mean that you know how to build a house. Someday, educators will wake up and realize that sentences are like footballs and hammers—knowing how to make them is *not* the same as knowing how to use them.

In recent years experts have complained that students are graduating from our public schools and colleges despite being unable to effectively communicate in print. To make matters worse, our academic community cannot agree on why such a sorry state of affairs exists.

Sentences express on paper the ideas you have in your mind. Of course grammar is important. No one could write well without mastering clauses, phrases, verbs, nouns, modifiers, and punctuation. But if that's all you know, you don't know what it takes to use writing to motivate someone else to accept your ideas. That is the essence of communication. Yet what role does motivational instruction play in the traditional writing course?

None whatsoever.

This is where *Don't State it . . . Communicate It!* comes in. You'll find on the following pages topics that are generally missing from English usage and stylebooks: how to achieve and maintain reader attention; how to identify and provide incentives that will motivate others to accept your ideas and to do what you want them to do; how to imply; how to sidestep what would otherwise be considered shortcomings in an argument; and how to customize writing to the needs of each reader. Most importantly, you'll learn how to view writing as others will view it, and how to edit accordingly.

Master these topics and you'll be able to *use* your grammatical skills to consistently score communications touchdowns.

1

WHY WRITE?

Compared to other forms of communication, writing offers many benefits. First, writing is permanent documentation. Tape recording is not always possible or acceptable, and the details of face-to-face or telephone conversations can be easily forgotten or confused in our memories. Anything written, on the other hand, is a permanent record that never forgets, never gets mixed up about the past, and never changes its recollection of what happened.

Second, writing does not depend on people being simultaneously available and interested in communicating. In-person conversation is possible only when two or more people are in the same place at the same time and are sufficiently interested in discussing a certain topic. Participants in a telephone conversation must be equally interested in talking to each other, but they must first have simultaneous access to an open phone line.

But maybe you don't have the time or money to travel so as to be in the same place as the person with whom you wish to communicate, nor does he. Or, maybe he's not near a telephone, or if he is near a phone, it's busy when you want to call; perhaps someone else is using your phone.

And even if those obstacles are overcome, just because you want to talk at a particular moment in time doesn't mean that you'll have a receptive audience. When someone visits you or calls to ask a question, you have to answer right then and there, if only to say that you can't talk for long. More often than not in such situations, however, you are dragged into a conversation while you're still thinking about what you were doing beforehand. Are you fully involved in that kind of conversation? Of course not.

Neither is the guy you interrupt with your visit or phone call. He might be polite and listen to your words, but he definitely won't give you his undivided attention.

Those problems don't exist when you write. As long as it meets its deadline, a letter, report, or proposal can be written at your convenience regardless of where the reader is or what he is doing when you are writing. Not in the mood to write at this time? Do you have something else to do now? Fine, put your writing down for the moment, and get back to it when you can.

The same applies to the person to whom you are writing. If the reader has other priorities or isn't near a telephone, what you have put on paper won't change. It can be read later, at the reader's convenience, instead of being forced on him while he was engrossed with something else.

A third advantage of writing is that it need not be done "off the top of your head." In conversation, you can't stop for a few minutes or put the other guy on hold every time you want to collect your thoughts instead of blurting out the first thing that comes to mind. If you correct yourself time and again, you'll make a poor impression. Unless you can think quickly and accurately while engaged in a conversation, you'll come across as tentative, incompetent, ignorant, or some combination thereof.

With writing, you can stop to think as often as necessary, as long as you don't take so much time that you finish too late to meet your objectives. You can type draft after draft until you're satisfied. All the reader sees is a finished document free of corrections or phrasing changes.

Writing is also more practical when communicating with many people. Theoretically, there is no limit to the number of people you can visit or telephone but when a message has to be communicated to more than a few people, talking with them can quickly become too time-consuming, prohibitively costly, or both.

Suppose you wanted to advise each of the ten thousand residents of your town that you were thinking of forming a civic association to promote better government, and that you plan to have an open meeting at the local school so that you can explain your purpose in greater detail, sign up members, and formally organize.

Ten thousand people can be spoken to personally, but doing so would take a long time. Even by telephone, that many people would take several weeks to contact unless you had dozens of volunteers making calls. You could try to spread your message by word of mouth, but that message would undoubtedly get reworded, if not distorted, every time it was told and retold.

A far better approach would be to write to each potential member, detailing your plans, the reasons for wanting to form an association, and the benefits to be accrued from banding together. The mailing will avoid the misinformation that would occur from word-of-mouth descriptions, while being faster and less expensive than telephoning and more practical than visiting each person on your mailing list.

Yet another advantage of writing is that it avoids unproductive emotionalism. Mad at someone? If he were in front of you, the intensity of your feelings might motivate you to say something you'd regret later on.

In contrast, writing allows you to safely "get it off your chest" and to "tell 'em off" but good. Having vented your emotional spleen, you can then cool off, tear up what you've written, and compose a letter that lets you express your grievances in a more constructive manner—one that will bring about a positive result instead of one that will further aggravate the situation.

Writing is also preferable in circumstances that in person might lead to emotions that would interfere with a productive exchange of ideas—informing people of bad news, putting forth a viewpoint that others might consider unreasonable, and mentioning anything that might be taken as a personal affront to someone's beliefs or life-style.

Then there's the problem of communicating with people who are headstrong and egocentric, who refuse to believe that your ideas might be better than theirs. Offer in person a recommendation that they change their ways and they're liable to become defensive, argumentative, and highly resistant to admitting that their ideas are anything short of total perfection.

Rather than going through all that nonsense, put your position in writing. Pile on a blizzard of incontestable facts, figures, charts, and analyses. Use a matter-of-fact tone that avoids the "my position versus yours" climate that would probably exist during an eyeball-to-eyeball confrontation.

Then wait a day or two, let the reader stew over your suggestions, and ask him whether he has had a chance to read them. If your facts and backup material truly are incontestable, you'll have a much better chance of succeeding than you would have had you relied on direct oral arguments.

Lastly, writing lends legitimacy to your message. Information in print is treated with great respect, particularly if it is typed on fine stationery with your name and address printed with raised letters.

With written communications, people see more than words; they see images. Fine letterhead stationery and crisp, clean typing have the image of success. Job titles and professional identifications further reinforce that image. And if you project a successful image, many people will assume that what you say is legitimate and valid.

To illustrate this point, imagine two letters typed on the same letterhead using the same typewriter. One says nothing below the signer's name, while the other says "President." Which letter would carry more weight?

Many companies are owned, staffed and operated by a grand total of one person. Most people, however, think that firms having presidents also have vice-presidents and large staffs. Such an assumption is unwarranted. All you need to be a president is a few dollars, a company name no one else is using, and access to a good printer. As far as the rest of the world is concerned, you will then be as legitimate as anyone else in print.

Imagery of this sort cannot be created over the telephone, and to create it in person can be quite costly. Fine clothes and traveling can be far more expensive than the cost of a decent letterhead. Beyond that, we all have a "Hollywood" image of what executives should look like. Do you look the part? Can you play the role? It's easy in writing, but for many people quite difficult in person.

The Drawbacks of Writing

There are, however, some primary disadvantages of writing. One is that it is indirect and relatively impersonal. Writing does not permit ideas to flow directly from person to person. The thoughts in one individual's mind must first be put on one or more sheets of paper which must then be delivered to an intended recipient. That person then has to read and interpret what's on that paper. Responses take the same route in reverse.

All this is too impersonal in some instances. People may be uncomfortable in completing an agreement or transaction without personally meeting you. Convincing someone to hire you or to spend a great deal of money buying your products or services, for example, is not likely to happen if all you do is write.

Another disadvantage of writing is that it is slow. The spoken word can be transmitted instantly. So can written materials, but only if you have access to telecopying or telegraph equipment. Before being conveyed to others, however, written information has to be composed, and that never happens instantly. A well-written letter can easily take a couple of hours to put together.

After that, it must then be delivered, it must wait its turn to be read among other written information delivered to the same person, and if that person isn't in when it arrives, it must wait for him.

Replies to written communications may take as little as a few hours, but they are more likely to take at least a day and, in some instances, two days to two weeks. Can you wait that long?

Writing has limited forcefulness. Being slow and indirect, writing lacks forcefulness compared to spoken communications. In person and via the telephone, communications permit a spontaneous "give and take" that allows you to immediately respond to questions, to counter resistance and to pour on arguments that will pressure people into seeing things your way.

Using the spoken word, in many instances, also allows you to interrupt. Doing so may be in bad taste, but it *will* command the other person's attention. Depending upon how forceful you are, speaking will allow you to keep that attention as long as you need it.

Written communications don't have that kind of impact. People *can* be motivated by written communications, but depending on how much convincing is necessary to overcome their resistance to your ideas, you may find that a written argument may take you to a point beyond which further progress cannot be made without a more direct form of impressing your thoughts on others.

You can also get and keep someone's attention with writing, but words on paper don't speak for themselves; when they arrive in the mail, they compete with other mail and with whatever else is going on while that reader is trying to read. Your message in writing may be just what readers want to see, but unless you know how to grab and keep their attention, they may not see it as quickly or as emphatically as you would like.

Supplementing

Just because you have no time to spare doesn't mean you can't write. Call or visit people if you're in a hurry to communicate with them, but don't hesitate to write afterward to confirm what was or was not said and agreed upon.

Similarly, a need for tough negotiating or convincing does not mean that writing can't help. You can write first and follow up later in person or over the telephone, you can use writing to document your thoughts and the thoughts of others, and you can write to keep people abreast of what's happening—all in a planned, unemotional manner.

Accordingly, writing can best be viewed as only a part of an overall communications effort. By itself, writing can't meet every communications goal in every situation, but it can help to supplement other forms of conveying and exchanging information and ideas.

But—and a big "but" it is—writing will work for you only if you realize that it is more than stating words on paper; words and sentences are merely a means to an end; the objective is to motivate others to accept your ideas. The following chapters will help you look at writing in that light, to set realistic objectives for what you write, and to meet those objectives as effectively and forcefully as possible.

2

TRANSFERRING IDEAS

Consult a dictionary and you'll probably find *writing* defined as a process by which people communicate by placing words and symbols on a surface to be read by others. The same dictionary will more than likely say that to communicate is to transmit, share or exchange information.

Those definitions are incomplete. Writing is not something we do because we want to provide others with reading material, and communicating is not the simple sending out and taking in of information. Unless we are in school, the purpose of writing well is *not* to show someone else how we excel in the skills of grammar and punctuation, but to have a specific effect upon what specific readers know, think and do.

Take Aim

When you write, you are very much in the same boat as the quarterback on a football team. If he throws left when his receivers are to his right, he makes no headway. Ditto if he throws to someone on the opposing team, to someone who is merely a spectator, or to a teammate who is not competent at catching the ball. Quarterbacks know that they can't just close their eyes and throw. To score or to make gains, they must get the ball in the right place at the right time, so that the right person can catch it.

So it is with communicating. When you want someone else to

accept or act upon an idea that starts out in your head, you must pass (in reality, transfer) the idea to that someone else. That's what communication is all about—transferring ideas. And like the quarterback throwing to the right receiver, communicators must aim for the right targets: specific people whose thinking and actions have to be influenced by the transfer of specific ideas. Without transferring the right ideas to the right people, we cannot communicate any more than a quarterback can gain yardage by throwing an incomplete pass.

Accordingly, writing consists of transferring ideas by putting words and symbols on paper to be interpreted by others in such a way that afterward, their knowledge or viewpoint coincides with yours, or you motivate them to take specific actions.

Malentendu

"Ingemination is boring." Only someone with an exceptional command of English would, without going through a dictionary, be able to translate the sentence into meaningful terms: "Repetition is boring."

Now that you have seen both versions, which conveys an idea and which will mean nothing to most readers? *Ingeminate* isn't even in most dictionaries. The word is properly used in the previous example, and the original sentence is grammatically correct, but the sentence is useless if its objective is to communicate with a reader who is not familiar with obscure, yet legitimate words. You must therefore make every effort to make certain that the people to whom you write can and do understand what you are saying. Readers will not be receptive to accepting a transfer of ideas if they must first look up the meaning of your words. Why should anyone be receptive to doing that?

The same applies to scientific jargon and acronyms (words derived from the first letter or two of each of a series of words). Unless you are positive that your reader knows, understands and remembers the meaning of your terminology, either define them or don't use them at all. Otherwise, you run the risk that people will simply not bother to decipher what you have said.

Ideas cannot be transferred to a reader who hasn't the foggiest notion of what you mean. Yes, people will look up meanings on occasion, but they are more likely to guess, to make the wrong interpretation, and as a result, to misconstrue. When that happens, you will have created a *malentendu*: "a misunderstanding."

Motivation

As the field general of his team, a quarterback need only instruct a receiver to be at a certain place on the field at a certain time to catch a pass. If that receiver is any good, he'll be there when the ball arrives. A writer, on the other hand, cannot tell people to look up words, to be receptive to certain ideas or to take actions requested in print. Short of using hypnosis, there is no effective way to transfer ideas by merely telling people what to do or think.

What you *can* do is to show people how they can benefit by being receptive to your ideas and by taking the actions you have requested. How do you do all that? You motivate.

Motivation is the art of getting people to believe that what you want them to do or think serves their own self-interests. Human beings will not think or act in a manner they perceive to be contrary to those interests, so if you want to transfer ideas to anyone, you had first better figure out what that person wants. Only then can you plan your strategy accordingly.

Whenever asked to read documents, accept ideas or take actions, each of us instinctively asks the same question: "What's in it for me?"

Here's another way of asking that question. "What do I get out of reading, accepting and acting on these ideas?"

Look closely and this question becomes three questions.

1. Why should I read this?
2. Why should I believe this?
3. Why should I do what the writer says I should do?

Writers who do not anticipate these three questions are poor communicators. People do not read a letter merely because it is sent to them; they read and later accept ideas only when they think they have something to gain by doing so; otherwise, nothing will be read and no ideas will be transferred.

Incentives

In the sense used here, an incentive is an opportunity to achieve some benefit or gain—a "carrot" held out by a writer to motivate a reader. People will take certain actions or think certain thoughts only if they are offered incentives in one or more of the following categories:

- an immediate tangible reward
- the promise of future tangible rewards in return for current actions
- immediate or future intangible rewards (such as recognition, praise, or love) that meet one of their basic needs as a human being
- a chance to take large or even small steps toward meeting their life objectives
- security from that they consider to be undesirable

TABLE 1 INCENTIVES TO USE IN WRITING

OFFER THE OPPORTUNITY TO

Attain power over others
Save face
Achieve recognition or prestige
Partake in an enjoyable activity
Defeat an opponent
Recoup a loss
Receive affection or praise
Be associated with someone they enjoy, can control, who will protect
    their interests, or from whom they can learn information of interest
Advance their career
Return a favor
Be a leader or trend setter
Witness a special event
Visit a special location
Become famous
Acquire something of value
Do something no one else has done
Join an elite group
Lose weight
Improve their health
Do something they've always wanted to do
Make a sale
Get a job
Save money, make more money
Protect their property or investment
Receive an award
Get something for nothing or almost nothing
Get revenge
Impress their boss, spouse, friends and so forth
Learn something of interest
Have fun
Help their children, parents, spouse, friends and so forth
Become more attractive
Pay less taxes
Hire better employees
Live longer
Become a better lover
Become better prepared for the future
Help their country, political party, synagogue, church and so forth
Become physically, emotionally, or financially stronger
Get ahead

Be happier
Gratify a basic instinct

OFFER THE OPPORTUNITY FOR SECURITY AGAINST

Failing
Being fired
Losing their money or property
Financial ruin
Pain
Paying too much
Death
Being left out
Missing out on an opportunity to make money, to buy at a bargain
    price, to purchase a unique item, to meet a special person and so
    forth
Unforeseen costs they can't cover
Accidents
Mistakes
Getting inferior quality
Looking or acting foolish
Underestimating risks
Overestimating chances for success
Deciding too early or too late
Trusting someone who doesn't deserve their trust
Hiring or firing the wrong person
Overlooking important facts
Making a bad investment
Being embarrassed
Hurting a friend or loved one
Going to work for the wrong employer
Being rejected
Not being able to provide for their family
Being ridiculed
The unknown

A list of typical specific incentives is shown in Table 1, but the table is by no means all-inclusive. The beauty of incentives is that they are limited only by your imagination and by your knowledge of what will be likely to get a reader "turned on." Once readers get the impression that reading a document will provide them with an attractive incentives package, that document will get at least a quick once-over. If the document is convincingly written and if the incentives powerful enough, idea transfer will be nonstop.

The danger with incentives is that you may dwell on what you think *should be* an attractive incentive, while not being nearly as concerned with finding out what the reader thinks *is* an incentive. In determining what to write, however, nothing should be offered as an incentive unless it is known to represent a compelling benefit from the reader's point of view. People will accept a transfer of ideas only on the basis of what *they* think is important, not what some writer thinks is important.

Getting someone to be receptive to reading, accepting and acting on your ideas is a variation on the old "I scratch your back, you scratch mine" routine. In return for doing or thinking as you request, readers expect access to certain benefits.

The Anatomy of a Decision

Before taking a conscious action—even one as simple and innocent as reading a short letter—individuals must first decide that doing so is in their best interests. The same applies to the mental action of accepting a new idea; first we think about the idea, then we decide whether it is acceptable.

My earlier book, *Throw Away Your Résumé*, contains an analysis of how people think and react to written job applications. Your objectives in writing may have nothing to do with getting a job, but your readers, being human, use the same thought processes no matter who they are and regardless of what you want them to do or believe. Those processes have four elements that compete with each other for the control of decisions: the decision maker's beliefs, instincts, emotions, and intelligence.

Beliefs are what a person thinks is true *before* reading what you have written. Included in beliefs are opinions, prejudices, or preferences on business, social, religious, political, economic, scientific, or other matters. Often ingrained in our minds for years, beliefs guide our thinking as to what is right or wrong, good or bad, and important or trivial.

People will accept an idea only if it is consistent with what they believe to be true. To communicate, you therefore have to know your readers' beliefs and to present your argument in such a way that you appear to agree with them. If that isn't possible, your position must not conflict with their beliefs. You'll learn more about these matters in chapters 4 through 6.

"Changing" a person's mind on a particular matter alters his beliefs on that matter, but you'll never change someone's viewpoint by attacking it. People modify their thinking only when they are given new information or a new way of looking at things.

Every individual has a different mix of beliefs, but some opinions are fundamental. Most people, for example, think that typewritten letters on quality stationery have credibility, whereas handwritten scribblings on scrap paper are the mark of someone who is highly unprofessional. Which image do you want to convey?

Instincts are compulsive drives that are an integral part of a person's way of life. In extreme cases, people can be consumed with the urge to gratify one or more of their instincts. Typical instincts include the need to—

> have control over others;
> know (curiosity);
> be attractive to others;
> gloat;
> save face;
> defeat competitors;
> be accepted by others;
> be safe and secure;
> be confident in one's own decisions;
> provide for spouse, children, and parents;
> grasp for opportunities;
> be praised, loved or idolized;

be rich or famous or both;
succeed;
help others in need;
enjoy life and be happy.

All people have the same instincts, but different needs predominate in different individuals. Some readers are so preoccupied with meeting a particular need that you can easily motivate them by providing them, as an incentive, with an opportunity to gratify that need.

Advertisers know the importance of motivating readers. We've all seen ad headlines like,

SAVE 40% ON YOUR HEATING BILL THIS WINTER

Upon seeing that line, people who pay for heat will be compelled to read further to find out what the "catch" is. Why would they be compelled? Two reasons: their need to know, and their need to be economical. If those needs are strong enough and the deal good enough, they may even be motivated to do just what the writer wants them to do.

Emotions can completely cloud a reader's thinking, so they must be channeled in a direction that will accelerate, rather than detour, a writer's motivational objectives. Typical emotions that writing can evoke are pride, anger, hate, love, loyalty, guilt, shame, envy, despair, hope, trust, and fear.

Love letters should, of course, inspire love; hate mail, if that's your thing, should be designed to generate hate and anger. Letters written to raise money for charities, on the other hand, can arouse sympathy, shame, and guilt in a triple-barreled attack designed to heighten a reader's instinctive need to help others.

One of the most versatile emotions is hope, which is the optimistic anticipation of achieving gains, of making the right decisions, or of choosing the lesser of two evils. Offer hope and you provide readers with a feeling that all is not lost, that there *is* a way to get what they want, and that what you have in mind can meet their objectives. Hope is an "escape clause" that you offer to readers in return for merely accepting your ideas and acting on those ideas in the manner you have prescribed.

Suppose a finance company was having difficulty getting a certain Mr. Martin to make payments on his auto loan. Would the following letter convince him to pay up?

> In light of your failure to make the last two payments on the automobile you financed through us, we are taking immediate steps to repossess your car. You are advised that such action on our part is in full accordance with state laws, and that we will not hesitate to prosecute should you in any way interfere.

This letter wouldn't convince Martin to do anything except possibly to hide the car before it can be taken away. Why should he do anything else? The letter tells him that the car *will* be repossessed; no escape clause is presented that would prevent his losing the car, and he certainly is given no reason to pay what he owes.

To get the money, a more productive approach would be to say:

> In light of your failure to make the last two payments on the automobile you purchased through us, we shall repossess that automobile unless satisfactory arrangements are made to bring your account up-to-date by payment of $452.64 within seven days.
>
> You are advised that such action on our part would be in full accordance with state laws, and that we will proceed without hesitation if we do not hear from you immediately.

Now, he has an out. There *is* something he can do to stave off disaster: Pay up.

Fear is the most powerful emotion of all. It can cause a reader to believe that something bad will happen or that something good will not happen. The problem with fear is that when backed into a corner, people may take drastic actions of an unpredictable nature. If you choose to generate fear, the next step is to follow up with hope that will channel reader actions to a direction suitable to your objectives. This is what was done with the second letter to Mr. Martin.

Finally, all written communications must generate trust. If we do not trust people, we will not believe what they say, and we certainly will not accept their ideas. Say anything that is perceived by readers to be untrue, phony, implausible, or contrary to their best interests, and you generate suspicion, which usually provides incentives sufficient to crumple your ideas on top of the trash heap.

Intelligence is the most misunderstood factor in the decision-making process, but neither you, your readers, nor anyone else can think on the basis of logic alone.

Intelligence can best be described as the ability to logically apply knowledge and experience to new situations. In other words, intelligence is the tool with which we use our beliefs to evaluate information made known to us for the first time. Yes, some readers are more intelligent than others, but each reader has different beliefs. The information you provide to a reader can therefore not be viewed in a vacuum of sheer logic, but rather in context with that reader's prior thinking and knowledge. As an example, Leonardo da Vinci, who had one of the most logical minds in history, would not have been able to understand this book; he did not learn how to read English.

Intelligence can also be curtailed by a writer's failure to provide enough information for a reader's logic to be implemented. No matter how logical your ideas may be, readers will never respond if you neglect to advise them of your name, address, or telephone number. But that's not all; instincts and emotions can hamper one's ability to be intelligent.

Typographical errors, for example, can murder anyone's logic. If you received a letter from someone saying that he had "information of hreat importance to your financial future," you would probably be leery because there is no such word as *hreat*. The message would be clear—the writer obviously meant "great," but the typist hit *h* rather than *g*. Those letters are next to one another on the typewriter keyboard, so the mistake is easy to make.

But you are not being asked to evaluate a secretary. The writer wants to manage or invest your money. Could you *trust* your finances to someone who could not spot a mistake as simple as "hreat"? You might, if you were willing to conclude that expertise as a proofreader has nothing to do with fiscal skills. On the other hand, were you concerned about the writer's ability to accurately read the financial news and stock reports, you might want nothing to do with him. If your instinct to be safe was strong enough, you would stay as far from him as you could, no matter how logical his proposal was.

One last fact about intelligence is that what may be logical for one person might be idiotic for another. A twenty-thousand-dollar tax-deductible contribution may be a great idea for people with large cash holdings, but would there be any logic to such a contribution for people who had to sell everything they owned to raise the money? Obviously not; those people would be logical only in rejecting the idea. Same logical proposal, same idea, but different readers with different circumstances. An intelligent course of action for some would be irrational, if not impossible, for others.

Combinations

One specific belief, instinct, or emotion can often dominate the way a reader reacts to incentives offered in writing. More frequently, however, decisions are made on the basis of a combination of factors, any one of which can help or hurt depending upon the skills of the writer.

Imagine writing a proposal geared at motivating a prospective customer to buy from you rather than from his current supplier. Your argument could be that you offer equal quality at lower price, or more value for the same price.

If the prospect has been buying from his current source for some time, he may *believe* that he is already getting a good product at a good price. He may therefore already be gratifying his *instincts* to be economical. Having become accustomed to one supplier, he may *trust* that supplier and therefore also feel *instinctively* safe with that supplier. Before you write, he accordingly sees no *logic* in looking around for another source. Beyond that, he may also feel a sense of *loyalty* to vendors who have served him well over the years.

When you come on-the-scene, you are an unknown, and the prospect has no prior beliefs on which to evaluate you. Can you be trusted? How much of a risk are you compared to the people with whom he has been dealing? If he cuts off his current source and you don't deliver as promised, what will he do then?

In opening up new accounts, a good sales manager will realize that customers may be reluctant to switch overnight from a known to an unknown supplier, and that personal ties may exist between customers and the salespeople with whom they have been working. The most productive sales ploy is therefore to say nothing about the current source (knocking a customer's friend may needlessly arouse the wrong emotions), to be very strong in offering price/quality benefits (to appeal to the customer's instinctive need to be economical and successful), and to offer to start out by providing only a small portion of the customer's needs. That way, Mr. Customer is offered an opportunity to try out what looks like a better deal (appealing to his instincts to improve his business) in such a way that he need not fear the minor risk it represents.

To motivate in this or any other situation, you have to deal with *all* possible factors. How you label any one factor is not important; should you consider something an instinct when it is actually a belief, you'll pay no penalty. But if you miss a factor, you may fail to identify the right incentives. Everyone has a price—a mix of incentives that will result in the action you want. Identify and provide the right mix, and you can't lose. Offer the wrong mix, however, and you cannot win.

3

THINK BEFORE YOU WRITE

Regardless of what you say or how you say it, you will always get results, but that isn't good enough. The question is whether you will get *good* results.

You will not get what you want from writing unless readers come to the conclusion that you are offering what they want. With the right advance planning, the difference between what you write and what you should be writing can be minimized if not eliminated.

Setting Objectives

The first step in the planning process is to set your objectives. This is done by asking yourself a few critical questions and demanding some specific answers:

1. What do I want to happen?
2. What do I want my readers to believe?
3. What do I want my readers to do?

Don't settle for vague answers. In setting objectives, the old expression "Mind your *p*'s and *q*'s," would be better stated as "Mind your *w*'s and *h*'s," because several questions must be asked with respect to any objective you come up with:

1. What do I want?
2. Why?

3. Where?
4. Which one?
5. Whose?
6. When?
7. What kind?
8. How?
9. How many or how few?
10. How much or how little?
11. How often?
12. How good or how bad?
13. How big or how small?
14. How difficult or how easy?

And these are just the start. Do you care whether the reader takes any liberties with your instructions? Which liberties are acceptable to you? To what extent are your instructions critical? Important, but not crucial? Of interest, but not necessarily important?

When you write a sales letter, what response do you want? A call or letter asking for more information? A telephone order based on credit card payment? A written order based on credit card payment? A written order with check enclosed? A call or letter asking you to make a sales call in person? All of the above?

OK, so you're not writing a sales letter; do you want someone to accept a new idea, to meet you someplace, to vote in your favor or to stop sending letters to your old address? Fine—which idea? Where do you want to meet? When? Which vote do you mean? What was your old address? Your new one?

Define and describe all your objectives as precisely as possible. If you want your business to grow, saying that you seek *more* sales is meaningless. How much more will satisfy you? Ten percent? Twenty? Fifty? Over what time period would you like this growth? Six months? Six years?

If you don't know *exactly* what you're after, neither will your readers!

Reader Circumstances

Once your objectives are established, the next step in planning is to determine the impact of the reader's circumstances on the situation. This can be done by assessing reader strengths and weaknesses according to six factors:

- Benefits. What gains will the reader reap upon acceptance of your ideas? Can you promise any additional benefits? To what extent will the reader think that what you offer is necessary and important?

- Risks. What harm or loss might be perceived by the reader as being inherent in your argument? To what extent can the reader afford to suffer those risks? What can you say to calm any fears associated with those risks?

- Resources. Does the reader have the skills, money, equipment, and so forth, necessary to do what you want? If not, can you show how he can obtain what is necessary? If not, your ideas may be rejected by default.

- Alternatives. What other choices does the reader have? Try to show how your approach offers fewer risks and more and greater benefits.

- Time Pressures. How can you make a case for convincing readers that delays will be costly to them? What penalty can you impose on a slow acceptance of your ideas?

- Reader Objectives. What does the reader want? Can you provide it? People will act and change their minds only to meet their own objectives, not yours.

To put reader circumstances in perspective, ask yourself some more questions and remember to be specific in coming up with answers:

1. What is the reader's current point of view on the subject about which you are writing?

   - contrary to yours? (in which respects?)

   - same as yours? (there must be some differences—what are they?)

   - neutral

2. Which reader beliefs will you have to change?

3. What objections might readers have to your proposal?

4. What can you say to overcome those objections?

5. Which beliefs and instincts will work in your favor?

6. Which incentives will you have to promise?

7. Which incentives *can* you promise?

8. Is the reader likely to be cynical?

9. How can you build trust?

10. Which other emotions should you evoke?

Be honest and objective in dealing with these questions, and you will be able to get a preview of how to proceed and whether your objectives are realistic. You may find that there is too much of a mismatch between what you can offer and what you have to offer to meet your goals. But that doesn't necessarily mean that all is lost; you can always address your message to different readers who have different circumstances, you can modify your objectives, and you can even improve your ability to offer more and better incentives.

Put Writing In Its Place

Make certain to distinguish between your overall objectives and those that can be met with written communications. Take another look at chapter 1—what role can good writing play in achieving your goals? Which objectives, on the other hand, will require the speed of a telephone call and which can be met only by a face-to-face conversation?

In many situations, several types of communications are required to meet an overall objective. Even if writing can do part of the job, it may therefore not be able to do the whole job. A letter may therefore have to be preceded or followed up by a telephone call or visit, and it may have to be followed up by one or more additional letters.

As people decide whether to accept or reject an idea, their thinking progresses through seven steps:

1. finding out about your idea
2. becoming interested in your idea
3. seriously considering your idea
4. weighing pros and cons (potential gains versus potential risks)
5. looking at or asking for better or alternate incentives
6. accepting or rejecting your ideas
7. acting on your idea if they accept it

Each of these steps must be looked at as an objective in itself. Can you move a reader's thinking through all these steps with a single letter, report, or proposal? Or, can one document be expected to propel that thinking only part of the way? Which part?

Getting someone to buy a vacation home, for example, cannot be accomplished solely on the strength of anything in writing—people will want to see real estate before they buy it. But a single document *can* get potential buyers through steps 1 and 2 by acting as an appetite whetter rather than as a request for cash and a firm purchase commitment.

In addition to meeting an overall objective, every document must therefore be written to motivate reader thinking through one or more specific steps in the decision-making process. So put writing in its place, decide what those steps are for each document you write, and design that document to do nothing else.

All Intents and Purposes

Not only does every document need an objective, each paragraph and sentence needs one also. If there is no purpose to a sentence, why write it? If there is a purpose, what is it? Typical purposes are to inform or to express an opinion. Let's look at these and more purposes.

To inform is to provide information. All sentences inform to one degree or another, but if all you do is to inform, you have an effect only on what people know. Keep in mind that knowing what you want is not the same as agreeing with it, which in turn is not the same as doing it.

To express an opinion is to inform readers of your beliefs.

To explain is to justify your information and to give the reasoning behind your opinions and conclusions.

To convince requires going a step beyond explaining. In explaining, you say why *you* believe certain ideas to be valid, but is your opinion of validity by itself sufficient motivation for a reader to form the same opinion? Not always; most people will instead ask: "What's in it for me?" Convincing therefore means informing, explaining and providing incentives.

To change a belief is to "change" someone's mind by virtue of what you say and how you say it. This is a form of convincing in which readers are motivated to accept an expressed or implied contention that more incentives are available with the new belief than with the old one.

To illustrate is to explain by using one or more examples.

To elaborate on another sentence a writer must add more information on the same aspect of the same topic as covered in the previous sentence. The sentence you are now reading elaborates by informing you that elaborative sentences are described in more detail in chapter 7.

To evoke an emotion is dangerous unless it's the right emotion vented in the right direction. What do you want your reader to feel? Toward whom or what? Will you get your way if the reader gets mad at himself? At you? Remember to create trust and to use hope and fear in constructive proportions.

To express an emotion of your own is fine as long as you do so in a mature, specific manner without ranting and raving. If you are upset, say so: "I'm upset." But then say why. If you expect the reader to take action to cause the upset to go away, describe that action.

To gratify instincts is easy, but sometimes too easy. Whose instincts are involved? Are you writing to get something off your chest and to satisfy your own instincts, or to provide readers with opportunities to meet their own needs? The difference is one of talking to yourself versus communicating with others.

To request information is to ask questions that will motivate a reader to get back to you with specific answers.

To provoke thought, the most typical technique is to pose a rhetorical question—one that will get the reader to think rather than to reply. Can you spot a rhetorical question when you see one? If not, read the preceding sentence again.

Thought can also be provoked by using sentences and paragraphs that imply, rather than assert, facts or beliefs.

> I am certain that you would be interested in knowing where your husband was last Thursday night, and what he was doing there with whom.

Used as the opening line of a letter, this example might, in the minds of many readers, immediately generate images of extramarital activities with an attractive female. Yet no such activities were described, nothing of an illicit nature was mentioned, and the gender of "whom" was not specified. Yes, the writer here is expressing an opinion relative to the certainty of a reader's interest in her husband's whereabouts, but the real purpose of the sentence was to create an image that would intrigue the reader into finding out what the writer had to say.

Provoking thought and creating imagery through implications are covered in chapter 4.

To confirm is to document information already known to the reader, and to make certain that neither of you forgets important details. You can confirm facts, your opinions about those facts, or your understanding of the reader's opinions. You will also learn in chapter 4 how, by using implications, to give the impression of confirming facts while actually stating your opinions.

To remind is to confirm while asking for action; for instance, urging someone to attend a meeting, and then repeating the previously announced time, date, and place.

To summarize is to draw conclusions from (or make synopses of) information that preceded or follows.

To use transitions one uses words, expressions, or sentences to show relationships between adjacent ideas and thereby to follow the train of thought within a paragraph or between paragraphs. The following example uses no transitions:

> A recognized authority on automotive engineering, Mark Harris, has authored a textbook on the evolution of the passenger car, and fourteen magazines have published his articles on highway safety and tune-up tips.

His book on British colonialism is regarded as the most complete study published in recent years on nineteenth-century international commerce.

The first paragraph here is quite clear. It *informs* us of Harris's expertise in the automotive field and *explains* using examples that *illustrate* his accomplishments, the validity of his status as a recognized authority. The second paragraph is equally clear, *informing* us of his book on British colonialism.

That second paragraph, however, comes as a surprise. After opening with a strong story about Harris's reputation in one area of endeavor, the writer would have surprised no one if the second paragraph went on to say more about what else Mr. Harris did in that same field. Instead, we are all of a sudden told what he did in an unrelated field. Why? What is the point of talking about cars and then detouring out into left field to discuss nineteenth-century international commerce?

As you will see in chapter 5, the impact of a document suffers whenever readers are presented with opportunities to ask "Why?" or "What is the point of? . . ." In this case, those questions need not be asked if two transitions are added:

A recognized authority on automotive engineering, Mark Harris has authored a textbook on the evolution of the passenger car, and fourteen magazines have published his articles on highway safety and tune-ups. *But Harris's writing is not limited to subjects such as spark plugs, tires, and transmissions.*

His book on British colonialism, *for example,* is regarded as the most complete study published in recent years on nineteenth-century international commerce.

These transitions would not be highlighted in normal writing, but they are italicized here so that you can easily spot them and see that none of the original words has been changed or deleted. Comparing the two versions of the story about Mr. Harris, you can also see that the transitions add no new information; the original version was clear in indicating that he wrote on topics outside the automotive field.

The difference between the versions is that with the transitions added, we do not have to ask why the British colonialism book is being discussed. Also, that end for the first paragraph provides a transition from one facet of Harris's writing to another. After reading that sentence, we have no reason to be surprised when a new field of interest is brought up. By neatly tying the paragraphs together, the transitions serve the additional function of helping the writer to identify Harris as a versatile writer.

Without the transitions, on the other hand, a reader might also have concluded that the objective was to describe Harris as a versatile person or as an individual of diverse interests. Perhaps those are all true, but the second version leaves no room for doubt—the specific objective is to hail the man's skills as a writer.

Transitions do not always add new information, and they don't have to be situated at the beginning or end of a paragraph, but when used wisely, they can be invaluable in improving the ease with which a reader can track your thought sequences.

To get action means motivating readers to do something. A request such as, "Let me know by Friday whether you will be here next Monday," instructs a reader that the "something" to be done is to get information to you by Friday. Alternatively, "Be here next Monday!" asks for attendance, not information. In both cases, the writer seeks action, but two different objectives call for two different actions. Do you know what actions will satisfy your objectives? If being someplace or accomplishing a specific task is what you require, don't merely ask for information, ask for your "something" to be done—where, when, and how you want it done.

Do not forget to explain and convince. Tell why the action must be done in accordance with your instructions, and offer incentives showing that yours is the course of action that offers the most gains and the least risks.

Compared to the intellectual steps required in decision making and idea acceptance, getting action involves motivating people to take physical steps. But if you think that anyone does something without first believing "it" to be beneficial, think again. And that does *not* mean beneficial to the writer; it means that writers never get any action without saying: "Here's what's in it for you."

Making It Happen

To illustrate the importance of paying attention to objectives and purposes, lets examine the case of Professor Smith, a respected member of a college faculty in New Jersey, and Professor Jones, who has a similar position with a university in the Pacific northwest. A year ago, Jones and Smith jointly received a grant to study ways of designing a new computer, but each man had his own ideas regarding how the project should proceed. Accordingly, they decided to first pool their ideas, and after that to work individually for several months, each pursuing the concept he thinks has the best promise. They agreed to keep each other advised of progress by means of letters and brief reports, such as this one written by Smith to Jones:

> My design will work better than yours. I therefore suggest that you immediately discontinue your research and concentrate on helping me to complete the hard disk design as soon as possible.

Will that get Jones to stop? Not on your life. This report raises more questions than it answers. Is Smith giving an opinion or is he relating some factual result? Smith's report summarizes and then attempts to get action. It does not explain, it does not illustrate, and it certainly will not convince. If anything, it may evoke anger: "My design will work better than yours" not only downplays Jones's design, but also his design capabilities. The only action this report would prompt would be a demand for an explanation.

Fortunately, Smith tore up this report before mailing it. Realizing that more details are in order, he composed a second draft:

> My design will work. I have checked my analysis with Professor Roberts, who has sent me a report showing new evidence proving that the hard disk approach will meet our goals without the memory limitations you have been encountering.
>
> I therefore suggest that you immediately discontinue your research and concentrate on helping me to complete the hard disk design as soon as possible.

That's better, isn't it? Smith is now starting to motivate. He explains *why* his design is better and only then does he ask for action. No reason here for Jones to take personal offense, but he would still have some questions. What about the work Jones has been doing? Is it worthless? Did Roberts test it? Can it be salvaged?

What Jones wants to know now is "What's in it for me to stop my research and help Smith complete his design?" To answer that question, Smith tears up the second draft and writes a third:

> My design will work. I have checked my analysis with Professor Roberts, who has sent me a report showing new evidence proving that the hard disk approach will meet our goals without the memory limitations you have been encountering.
>
> Although his earlier data indicated that currently available memory core materials would work with your approach, Roberts's latest research, which he considers more comprehensive, shows that what you are attempting would require use of alloys that are at present too costly to be commercially practical. A copy of his report is attached, along with my latest findings. Please feel free to contact me or him should you have any further questions.
>
> In light of these developments, however, I suggest that you immediately discontinue your research and concentrate on helping me to complete the hard disk design as soon as possible.

Now Smith has done it. He has informed, he has explained, he has illustrated (by attaching his latest findings and a copy of Roberts's report), and he has, by pointing out that Roberts's original data were misleading, gratified Jones's instinctive need to be justified in proceeding on a design that has proved to be impractical.

By using the grammatical tool—the transition—the author indicates that Jones's design would not be acceptable with currently available materials. Smith also offers hope that the design may be resurrected if new materials are available in the future. "What's in it for me?" is therefore a threefold combination: ceasing work on a design that has no immediate promise; starting work on one that does, and being vindicated.

Primaries and Secondaries

Smith's primary purpose in writing to Jones was to change the direction of a research program. To make that happen in a constructive manner, he had to inform, to illustrate, to explain, to convince and to change a belief. He also had to evoke hope and trust. Had he not made use of these secondary intentions, his primary objective would have been beyond reach.

Every written communication has primary and secondary intentions. If you were to write simply to remind people to attend a scheduled meeting, your primary purpose would be to refresh their memories, but you might also want your readers to—

- believe that they would benefit from attending;
- be motivated to perform advance preparations;
- be motivated to cancel or postpone conflicting appointments;
- be motivated to attend.

Can you remind and do nothing else? You can, but if your objective is maximum attendance by people who are enthusiastic and well-prepared, you must motivate, and that means you must convince, explain, *and* remind.

Which result is your primary intention? which purposes will get that result?

Objectivity

Objective has two meanings: Being objective means being able to look at yourself as others see you, and being able to look at others in a way that is not clouded by your prejudices; an objective is also a goal.

To be objective while setting goals, you have to make certain that what you say in writing is consistent with your actions, with the way you and your words are perceived, and with the way your readers look at the topic you are writing about. If you are not objective about setting objectives, you are likely to communicate nothing but confusion.

This is exactly what happened to Big Mike. Mike started his delivery business twelve years ago with a small amount of cash and a lot of self-confidence. He initially had to make all the big decisions himself, but as sales grew, he had to hire more and more people to handle the load. Now, he is worth millions and three hundred people are on his payroll, but he is miserable.

When business is slow, Mike sends out countless memos urging his people to come up with new ideas to stimulate sales. Down deep, however, he is terrified of new ideas because they are quite unlike those he used to build the business years ago. To make matters worse, he distrusts employees who do not do things the same way he would, but he never bothers to tell them what his way is. He fires off additional memos degrading his employees for making mistakes, while never saying what they should have done to avoid or prevent those mistakes. Most of his people are convinced that the only mistake they made was to work for him.

Big Mike's memos have zero impact. Most of the time, his employees have no idea what he wants, but they do know that keeping him informed is an invitation to be chewed out for doing things wrong. They also know that to make a suggestion to Mike is to have it turned down.

Should Mike change his ways? That's for him to decide. His instincts to call all the shots may get in the way of the sales he says he wants, but if methods are what really turns him on, he'd be better off to stop asking for the suggestion "targets" he has been demanding.

The problem with Big Mike's approach is that it creates an environment in which he and his readers have different objectives. He wants influence and a feeling of importance, whereas his employees want raises, job security, and the satisfaction of being able to contribute to the company's success.

Mike is no dummy; if he were, he would not have become a success in business. But success as a businessman does not qualify one to know anything about communications, written or otherwise. If Mike truly wanted results only, he would remove the lack of incentive for coming up with new ways to do things. He would not have to accept every idea, but he just might find a few that are better than his. Should methods be his true goal, however, he'll get better cooperation by telling his people exactly how he wants things done and promising to take the blame if his methods fail.

The world is full of guys like Mike. They're not objective enough to realize that what they want is something other than what they say they want in writing. Their deeds or spoken words communicate one message, and their writing says something else. As readers, we don't know which message to heed.

Are you a Big Mike? Do you say one thing on paper and another in person? Are you objective enough to know what you really want? Can you put your beliefs aside longe enough to visualize what you write as others will see it?

Targets Versus Methods

A target is a "what"—an end result such as taking a specific action. A method, on the other hand, is a "how"—the manner in which a result is accomplished. An objective can be either a target or a method, but you have to clearly define in your mind which one you want—the end or the means to that end.

In the case of Smith and Jones and their computer research, Smith's primary objective was a method—a particular way of designing the new computer. His secondary objective was a target—to get Jones to stop working on a design that was impractical. Big Mike, on the other hand, didn't bother to differentiate between targets and methods. He said he wanted targets in the way of new ideas, but his primary goal was control over the methods his people used to run the business.

How about you? Are you after an end or a means to that end? Whichever your preference may be, structure your writing accordingly, and don't forget to keep your reader's preference in mind. If a reader is interested in reaching a specific destination while you talk only about a new mode of travel, you'll be on entirely different wavelengths.

4

IMPLICATIONS

When evaluating written material of a nonfiction nature, we often have no way of knowing whether we are reading lies, bluffs, or distortions. Even if what we see is truthful, however, we don't know if it represents the whole truth or whether the writer has purposely or inadvertently left out information we would want if we knew it existed.

If the *whole truth* about any subject is defined as a totality of all valid and correct information pertaining to that subject, no document contains the whole truth. "Our meeting is scheduled for next Monday at 8:00 P.M." may be a truthful way to word a confirmation notice, but is it complete? Obviously not; a bad storm, a power failure, or another disaster could always cause a change in plans.

But do we then amend simple reminders by saying that the date may change if World War III intervenes? Do we include a ten-page list of other possibilities that might change the date, along with a two-hundred page book outlining the logic behind how the date might be rescheduled in each eventuality should Monday night not work out? While we're at it, we should probably send along a four-hundred page volume containing the biographies of everyone anticipated to attend, a thirty-page summary of meeting expenses over the past two years, and the architectural plans for the meeting hall.

Forget it! No one would read all that, and the confirmation would probably get lost in the midst of everything else. Besides, the purpose of confirmation is to confirm, so the best bet is to edit out (and perhaps never even write) the rest of the material. Will the readers get the truth? Yes. Will it be the whole truth? No. We never get the whole truth about anything.

Dishonest intentions and editing decisions aside, another limitation with the truth is that we may be reading something from a writer who is sincere, yet misinformed or mistaken. Should such a writer create a persuasive argument, we may not know until it's too late that we've been duped by a dope.

Another limitation of the truth is that it doesn't exist if it hasn't happened yet. When we decide whether to be motivated by a writer's urgings to accept ideas or to take actions, we are choosing between alternatives, basing our choice on the incentives available with each option. But instant gratification is rarely our reward; we make decisions now in anticipation of achieving benefits at some future time. We usually never know if we have chosen correctly.

The decision to be motivated is therefore based on guesswork; our guesses may have a solid foundation, they may be based on the best information available, and they may have the concurrence of everyone we know, but they are still guesses nonetheless.

What this means is that to the same extent that beauty exists in the eyes of those who behold it, truth exists in the minds of those who believe it. From the written word alone, we cannot tell truth from the writer's opinions, we don't know how much of the truth we are getting, and we have no way of telling whether what seems true today will still be true tomorrow.

Assumptions

When given incomplete information, computers have the good sense to stop computing. Humans aren't that smart; we start making assumptions when we run out of known truths. Using our experience and prior beliefs, we will assume what is true or false, right or wrong, and logical or illogical. The ability to make rational assumptions is what separates us from machines and from other animals.

It's easy; when confronted with the need to make a decision in the face of incomplete information, we simply "put two and two together" to arrive at what we believe is the true answer to our dilemma. If only life were really that simple!

Unfortunately, two plus two does not always equal four. As any third grader knows, $2+2=4$, but that answer is true only under very restricted circumstances. Conclusive proof has just been uncovered to indicate that two plus two can also be equal to six! That's right. *Two* quarters *plus two* nickels *is equal* in value *to six* dimes.

In truth, two plus two equals four only when a pair of one thing is added to another pair *of the same thing*. If different things are being added, two plus two can yield any number you want. If you thought the only true answer to be four, you were acting on the belief that a pair of something was being added to another pair of that thing. Where was that stated in the sentence about two plus two being equal to six? Sorry, but no such condition was stated there; you had to assume it.

Making unwarranted assumptions is the Achilles's heel of the human way of thinking. Aside from interfering with our logical capabilities by forcing us to deal with feelings such as love, anger, loyalty, trust, and hope; our emotions saddle us with intuitive feelings and impulsiveness, equally irrational compulsions that won't let us stop drawing assumptions about everything we hear, see and read. Some people are more impulsive or intuitive than others, but we all assume more than we should.

Perceptions

Start with one part incomplete truth, add a filler in the form of an uncontrollable tendency to make assumptions, mix in a heaping portion of preconceived notions and blend with a generous assortment of instincts spiced with emotions. Top it all off with a sprig of intelligence, bring to a head in a person's brain, and what you have is that person's *perception* of what is true, valid, and real.

In the sense used here, a perception is the truth as one person "sees" it. Occasionally, we perceive things as they are, but all too often what is perceived bears little resemblance to reality. When too much preconception and impulsiveness is mixed with too little intelligence and actual truth, the result is poor judgment.

Four separate truths pertain to every issue:

1. The absolute truth. Defined as a totality of correct information on what is, was, and will be, the absolute truth exists only in concept, but is unknown to both writer and reader.

2. Your perceptions. The truth as you see it.

3. A reader's starting point perceptions. This is the truth as the reader sees it before reading what you have written.

4. The same reader's final perceptions. After reading your words and ideas, this is what the reader will believe to be true.

Communication is a matter of shifting reader viewpoint from truth number 3 to a truth number 4 that will result in the acceptance of your ideas. Unless one of the reader's starting perceptions is that your viewpoint is highly valued, your perceptions are of no consequence to anyone but yourself, and the absolute truth never enters the motivational equation without being first massaged by personal interpretation.

The greater the "distance" between starting point and final perceptions, the more difficult it is to motivate someone to accept your ideas. Communication is therefore easiest when a reader sees little or no difference between those perceptions. How much difference is seen is a perception unto itself—one that is created by the manner in which a writer provides information, offers incentives and presents arguments.

The best evidence of this is the success with which advertising copywriters can motivate us to buy a multitude of products and services that in truth, are no better than the infamous brand X that all advertisers are forever knocking. Is there really all that much difference between competing brands? Is one really that much better than the other? Occasionally there are differences, but in the majority of instances, the only differences are those put in our minds by clever promoters who play on our perceptions.

If you have doubts about the impact of perceptions, take a good look at a product like shampoo. You'll find a wide assortment of brands—some costly, some inexpensive; some well-known, and some you never heard of. Yet unless a brand is formulated for some special purpose, it can be seen on the back of the bottle to have essentially the same ingredients as any other brand. Obviously, buying one rather than another is not a simple matter of truth in terms of which is better—the chemicals in one bottle perform according to the same laws of nature as the same chemicals in another bottle from another manufacturer. Brand preference is, however, a matter of perceptions.

Were truth the only factor in decision making, someone's mind could never be "changed" because the truth is the truth regardless of viewpoint and regardless of whatever arguments are presented. Perceptions *can* be changed because they are merely our impressions of the truth.

We do not look upon our perceptions as the opinions or preferences they really are, but rather as universal truths that we have been smart enough to recognize. This does not mean that all ideas are accepted with strong convictions or without some reservations. It does, however, mean that we are incapable of accepting any idea that we perceive as being wrong or as being the greater of the available evils. Even if we have reservations or doubts, once we decide, we will think as being correct only what we perceive as probably being correct, and take only those actions we perceive to probably represent the lesser of evils at our doorstep.

Infallibility

Not all perceptions are issue-oriented; some are associated with a reader's ego and self-image. Acceptance of new ideas often forces us to realize and possibly admit that one or more of our earlier perceptions was wrong. Depending upon the strength of their egos, some people cannot bring themselves to any such admission. Since they do not make mistakes and could not have been wrong, they won't change their minds regardless of what you say.

In the extreme, egocentric people act and think as if they had a corner on intelligence. Their perception is that no one else is capable of coming up with good ideas, so no matter what you say, they will assume that there is a loophole in your argument. These people will latch onto any thread of doubt just to preserve the perception of their own infallibility.

When people perceive their thinking to be infallible, they do not want to be confused with the facts, and they will be quite defensive if you say anything that even hints that they have goofed. You'll get a lot further by saying something to the effect that "You are correct, but here is additional information you should consider. . ." or "I understand your logic, but did you know that. . .?"

Uniqueness

Another ego-dominated perception is that each of us has needs that are uniquely different from those of anyone else. Yes, each person has a unique blend of personality traits, physical characteristics, abilities, and interests, but we all have the same basic needs.

In sales situations, each prospective customer perceives that he has different needs. As a collection of egos, each corporate organization perceives itself to be quite unlike any other organization in terms of what it needs to survive and to succeed.

The strict meaning of *unique* is "one of a kind" or "singularly unlike any other." In practice, however, unique is used to mean "very different." Are people and companies really all that different? Not as different as they think they are, since all organizations are run by human beings and most human beings have strong needs to be safe and to achieve maximum gain with minimum effort accompanied by little or no risk. Figure out what someone wants to be safe from, and you might get whatever you want merely by offering that particular kind of safety.

The important point about uniqueness is not whether people are or are not "one of a kind" but rather that they *perceive* themselves to be singularly unlike anyone else. So why burst their bubble? Taking on a reader's ego will put you at odds with a powerful adversary. Instead, tell your readers that you too see them as unique people who will not be satisfied with "one size fits all" suits, commonplace solutions to their problems, or conventional approaches to meeting their needs. Position yourself as offering a series of incentives that are ideas and actions that are not too little, and not too much, but custom-tailored to their perception of having exacting needs.

Belonging

One of our most fascinating character traits is that no matter how much we want to be unique, we do not want to be so different that we look or act like visitors from Mars. To a degree, everyone conforms to certain social norms, even those who egomaniacally drive to control everyone and everything.

Look at powerful business owners. They have more money than they'll ever be able to spend, they dominate the lives of hundreds if not thousands of employees, and they pretty much do as they please in their personal and business affairs. Yet how do they dress—any way they want? No. Most dress like a business executive is expected to dress. Men wear the traditional vested suit to work, complete with dress shirt and necktie.

Necktie? Of course! What an absurd frill. No one would be more productive by wearing a necktie, no profits are predicted on neckties, and people don't work harder when they are wearing neckties. So why are they worn?

They're worn because the wearers feel more appropriate with them on, and because some customers wouldn't feel right about doing business with a man who wasn't wearing a necktie. Those feelings may or might not be logical, but they are *perceived* to be logical and are therefore important.

Neckties are one form of many "everybody's doing it" perceptions that dominate our lives. They are also, in conjunction with other articles of clothing, a perception about the importance we attach to status symbols. Yes, we want to be different, but we do not want to be outcasts, so we exhibit our difference by doing things that are socially acceptable ways of being unique.

All this opens up many vistas for communicators. Can you convince people to take action because they perceive themselves to have certain "discriminating" tastes that are symbols of status? Can you motivate by showing them how others are doing something? Sure you can. All you have to do is to show them that you understand their needs and that you are providing an opportunity for meeting those needs in a socially proper manner.

Similarities

The key to communication is eliminating, in the minds of your readers, any perceived differences between their starting point perceptions and what you want them to believe as a final perception.

Convincing is largely a matter of concentrating on similarities as opposed to differences. Rather than trying to motivate someone to adopt drastically different thoughts, you'll find communication a great deal easier if you can create the impression that there's really not much difference between what readers think now and what you want them to think. Your job will also be easier if you can motivate readers to believe that there is a great deal of similarity between their objectives and the results to be achieved by doing what you want done.

Ideas and results do not have to be identical with what a reader may have in mind, but the greater the similarity, the less of a chance you are asking a reader to take by going along with you.

No one wants to be a guinea pig. Typically, people will perceive less risk and greater probability of success if what you want them to do has already been proven to work in a situation they believe is similar to theirs. If you claim some expertise or ability to get something done, readers will doubt your credibility unless you have a successful track record.

Concern about similarities is why companies in a particular field like to hire and do business with individuals and firms who know that field and who have been successful in it. More often than not, the truth of the matter is that the need for similarities is more imagined than real, but why get confused with reality when your readers are hung up on mere perceptions?

Use similarity perceptions to your advantage. Identify as many as you can and hit hard in emphasizing any and all areas in which what you are proposing coincides closely with what the reader has in mind.

Implications

Thoughts cannot be driven into anyone's head with a hammer or pumped into anyone's veins with a needle. People can be forced to take unpleasant actions and to adopt what they believe to be poor ideas, but only when they perceive the alternatives to be even worse. Persuasion by force, however, is often short-lived, since a person so motivated will also be compelled to find a way out and usually does.

But suppose you had a way of getting people to think what you want them to think—not because you're exerting force, but because they are human and cannot resist the temptation to "put two and two together" and draw conclusions about every smidgen of information they encounter. Suppose further that you don't even have to come out and say what you want them to think, but only to provide information in a manner that allows them to draw only those conclusions you want them to draw. That way, they feel no pressure and will be comfortable in formulating perceptions that seem to them to be logical and in their best interests.

Contrary to the old adage about not being able to get a horse to drink after leading it to water, people can be forced to accept ideas merely by leading them, with incomplete truths, to the point where they can form specific conclusions.

An implication is an unstated idea communicated by presenting information in such a way that someone else will conclude that the idea exists, is valid, and should be accepted. Such a conclusion is called an inference. Drawn partly on the basis of provided information and partly on the basis of our tendency to make assumptions every time we don't get the complete truth, inferences are made with regard to every aspect of written communications.

In contrast to implications, some sentences explicitly state the ideas the writer wants to convey, and no assumptions need be made by readers to understand what the writer means. A sentence such as, "This book has nine chapters," appears quite clear and requires no inferences to understand. Yet just because no inferences are required does not mean that no inferences will be made. Seeing "This book has nine chapters" here, for example, may cause you to infer that the sentence refers to the book you are reading now. In your eyes, the sentence would then be perceived as saying, "*Don't State It . . . Communicate It* has nine chapters."

If that is what you have inferred, you are not incorrect; this book *does* have nine chapters. But chances are you won't be satisfied with that. You might also have inferred that three other words have been implied, resulting in a complete meaning of, "*Don't State It . . . Communicate It* has *a total of* nine chapters."

Hopefully, you did not fall into the trap of assuming those three words to have been intended. Sorry, but you are now reading a book that has a total of *ten* chapters. To say that it has nine chapters is an incomplete truth, and to say that it has *a total of* nine chapters is a complete falsehood.

In the event that you did not draw the inferences just described, you are quite unusual. Most people would draw those inferences because they can't stop "reading between the lines" even when they have no business doing so. The same will happen with, "George is a lawyer."

This example seems to express the simple fact that someone named George is a lawyer. Is that all you see? Or, like most people, will you infer the following "facts" to also be true?

1. George is a human being; animals and things can be named George, but contrary to the opinions of some of us, only people can be lawyers.

2. George is a male. A female might be named Georgia but not George.

3. He is a college graduate. Otherwise he would not have gotten into law school.

4. He is also a law school graduate.

5. He has passed whatever bar examinations one must pass in order to practice law.

6. He does practice law as opposed to being allowed to practice law and deciding to do something else.

7. He earns a living primarily or solely on the basis of his knowledge and abilities in legal matters.

8. He works for a corporation, an organization, an institution, a branch of government, a law firm headed up by others, or his own legal practice.

9. He is at least twenty-five years old. Someone is unlikely to have graduated college and law school at an age appreciably younger than that.

But then again maybe this George became a lawyer years ago when bar exams were not required. Maybe he retired ten years ago and today deals only with a few clients on a part-time basis. Or, he may be a corporate chief executive who rarely does lawyering nowadays. Each of these maybes is as plausible as the nine inferences just listed, but upon seeing "George is a lawyer," most readers will conclude that the writer is talking about a man who currently practices law for a living. Yes, there are retired lawyers, lawyers who now do other things, and lawyers who practice only part of their time, but those are exceptions to the rule and we usually do not infer exceptions—we infer what we perceive is most probable.

We also use association to draw inferences. "Dr. Smith is not allowed to practice medicine in Nevada," for example, looks as if the good doctor has run afoul of the authorities in Nevada, but that isn't necessarily the case. We see "Dr." and associate it with "medicine" to infer that Smith is a medical doctor, but we don't know that. If Smith's doctorate is in economics, he will not be allowed to practice medicine anywhere!

Like all implications, these have four characteristics in common:

1. They all give the appearance of expressing facts.

2. Each contains one or more incomplete truths.

3. None includes any elaboration on mentioned facts.

4. Every one will lead readers to draw specific inferences.

Why Imply?

Your saying something does not make it true in someone else's mind unless he follows you on blind faith alone. Before "taking your word" for anything, people are likely to suspect your motives, your honesty, your understanding of their needs, the validity of your information, and your logic. As a result, you have to blast away with strong arguments loaded with evidence on your behalf. And even then, a reader's instinctive need to be safe may throw up a wall of defenses that prevent your transferring even the most logical ideas.

Sometimes, reader defenses are self-generated by an ego-driven refusal to be swayed by others, while on other occasions, well-meaning people establish for themselves certain criteria against which your arguments will be measured. Meet those criteria, and your ideas are welcomed; otherwise, you lose. No matter what the basis for their stubbornness, however, people are always guided by their perceptions of whether and how what you propose is consistent with their best interests.

By restricting yourself to expressing and fully explaining facts, you are attempting to deal on the basis of absolute truth. Unfortunately, however, this puts you at a distinct disadvantage since most readers function entirely on the basis of perceptions. Their goals are perceived, their criteria for idea acceptance are perceived, their concepts of reality and priority are perceived, and their sense of importance is perceived. They'll get confused with all your facts. You've heard of fighting fire with fire? Great—then fighting perceptions with perceptions should not be a surprising tactic.

When people infer similarity between what they believe you to mean and what they perceive is true and in their best interests, their defenses come down. That's when your ideas come in, and that's why implications are so powerful; the reader is forced to focus on meanings rather than on words, and if you imply effectively, those meanings will be just the ones you want.

Expectations

Readers do not base inferences on a literal interpretation of your words, but on what they expect your meaning to be. This is why, in the context of a sales letter, that, "We know how to get results," is never taken to mean, "We know how to get *trivial* results," or "We know how to get *poor* results," because those meanings would not be expected from a seller.

"We know how to get results" literally says nothing meaningful, since the type of results is not stated. Yet that sentence is always inferred to mean, "We know how to get *good* results."

But that's not all. Reader expectations are that good results are represented as being in store for them, not just for the writer. Furthermore, readers will expect that if someone knows how to get good results, he will, for a fee, translate that knowledge into action. Accordingly, the full inferred meaning is, "We will get good results for you."

That's a fine statement for building customer confidence in a proposal, but if you state it without implications, you may become legally liable for offering what amounts to a de facto guarantee. Implying gets the same message across without such exposure.

Speaking of guarantees, some manufacturers are thrilled to tell us that, "Our performance data is fully certified." They say this because many customers are thrilled to read it. But it means nothing. Certified by whom? To be what? To do what? As what? Literally, the sentence means that the data are genuine, but that's not the same as being guaranteed, which is what the majority of readers will expect it to mean.

Opinions

Since your opinions will, in the minds of most people, hold less weight than facts, you won't help your cause by basing your arguments on what you think is right or wrong, good or bad, important or trivial. Every time you stress that some viewpoint is a viewpoint and that it is *your* viewpoint, you put yourself in the position of having to provide all sorts of explanations and verifications to help transfer that viewpoint to the reader. If, however, you present the same information as if it were the gospel, it takes on added emphasis and credibility. Supporting evidence still may be required, but as backup rather than as justification for what you think. Accordingly, "I believe that your application will be rejected," will be more emphatic and definite when implied to be fact rather than opinion: "Your application will be rejected."

Is that a little too definite for you? Fine—take the edge off with, "Your application will most likely be rejected."

Implying is also a great way to brag without coming across as a braggart. In a sales letter or job application, there's nothing wrong with making claims, but people will be interested in what you offer them, not in how high an opinion you have of yourself. They may applaud self-confidence, but they have no way of telling whether it is justified or so much hot air. So let them draw their own conclusions. Be as factual as possible, imply more claims than you state and let inference take its course: "Sales have doubled since I took over five years ago. We now do business with every hotel in the state."

Had you written those sentences in the midst of a sales proposal or job application letter, you would have implied a host of inferences:

1. that your efforts have been directly responsible for the increase in sales

2. that you have successful experience in increasing sales to hotels

3. that you put procedures into effect that were more successful than those used previous to the time when you took over

4. that when you took over, the company you are with was not doing business with every hotel in the state

5. that you, the company you are with, or both have a good reputation among hotels in the state

6. that the company you are with has benefited by your having taken over

7. that you probably have one of the company's highest rankings as a salesperson

8. that had you not taken over, sales would not have doubled and the company would not now be doing business with every hotel in the state

9. that relative to the product or service you are selling, you understand the needs of hotels

10. that a doubling of sales represents a good performance

11. that you have been in charge continuously over the past five years

12. that you can and will continue to achieve results in the future

13. that you are still in charge and expect to remain in charge

14. that you are a worthwhile person with whom to be associated

15. that your company has grown continuously since you took over, and is still continuing to grow

16. that you do business primarily or only in the state

Starting with only twenty words, the two sentences we are looking at can therefore communicate almost that many facts combined with those that were actually stated to begin with. Are they facts? Who knows—perhaps the business quadrupled after your first year and has been going downhill ever since. Maybe your only contribution was in hiring a good saleswoman in each territory. It is even possible that everyone else in your business had done much better and that in your case, doubling sales was a mediocre performance. Each are possibilities that are not inconsistent with the sentences originally stated, but none would be inferred. Not every reader would infer all of the sixteen inferences either, but a typical reader would pick up on most of them.

Presuming that you start with true statements and lead readers to correct inferences, you can "say" more than you state, avoid coming across like a blowhard and make a great impression—

simply by giving people just enough information to draw inferences ... and nothing else. Elaborating, if it provides any ammunition for damaging the impression you have created, it should be avoided at all costs.

Optical Implications

Words are not the only way to imply meanings. Fine stationery and imprinted letterheads imply professionalism and success, a lack of errors implies attention to detail, and "proper" grammar implies education and professionalism. But also, incorrect spelling implies a lack of education, professionalism, or both; smudges imply sloppiness, and computer labels imply a mass mailing that is not personalized.

A bad impression on any of these counts can ruin the impact of any message. Equally damaging are inconsistencies between what people see and what you say. It's fine, for example, to imply offering personalized benefits by saying, "We have just what you want," but don't do it in a letter that looks like a photocopy that looks as if it were sent to everyone else in North America.

Lying

"Implying is a great way to lie without explicitly stating a falsehood."

What you have just read has been implied on several occasions earlier in this chapter, but not stated until now. It's true— implications allow you to distort and twist the truth any way you want.

The most effective writers are those who prepare good advertising copy. They can motivate large numbers of people to do and believe many things. To get their way, advertisers imply and in doing so often take liberties with truth and reality. But the good ones—those who stay in business—realize that no matter how tricky they may be in getting us interested in something, they must satisfy us. If they don't deliver as promised, word of mouth will bring them down even if the authorities don't.

Lincoln was right; you cannot fool people all of the time and you cannot, except in isolated instances, communicate on a foundation of distortions. Even beyond the obvious ethical considerations, lying or distorting facts is bound to get you into trouble in most situations. Written communications are too often accompanied by telephone and in-person conversations that would expose lies to cross-examinations that cut through to the truth.

But who says that you can't put your best foot forward by implying that what you are saying has only positive attributes? Who says that communications should be so complete that you have to voluntarily provide readers with reasons to reject your ideas?

As long as you have something legitimate to offer, there is no need to lie. The next chapter will show you how to use implications and explicit statements in combinations that are stronger and safer than creating your own fiction.

5

ALL POSITIVES, NO NEGATIVES

Congratulations! After twenty years of working for the same company, you have been promoted; you are now the new vice-president of sales and marketing. At first, you're thrilled with the new job, but then you realize that you're the person who is going to have to handle Phil.

Phil? The two of you joined the company together and for a while moved up the corporate ladder at about the same pace, but he is not as dynamic as he once was. He runs the company's largest regional office but his output is slumping. Competition is taking the lion's share of sales in his territory, and something has to be done to either light a fire under Phil or to replace him with someone else who will increase business in the area. Maybe you can hire the competition's regional manager out there; their business is booming.

Before now, you have thought of Phil as a personal friend; you've been to his house, he has been to yours, and you have shared a lot together over the years. You certainly won't find any enjoyment in being tough with Phil, and the thought of being forced to get rid of him is, to say the least, unpleasant.

But something has to be done to shake Phil up, so you write, saying:

Dear Phil:

This is a difficult letter to write because you and I have been friends and business associates for twenty years. Now, however, sales in your territory are slumping badly despite the fact that our competitors (and each of our other regions) are doing quite well.

What are you going to do about improving your performance? If a turnaround in sales does not occur soon, we will be forced to take drastic action if only as a last resort.

Please advise your thoughts on this matter as quickly as possible.

Will Phil be shaken up by such a letter? Not at all! The first statement he sees refers to your personal relationship. Later, he sees that you will take drastic action only as a last resort. Still later, he sees that you have asked for his thoughts "as quickly as possible," a request hardly indicative of a crisis. The overall tone of the letter is one of asking for a favor at Phil's convenience, and of using a long-standing friendship as the motivation for providing that favor. If Phil has any smarts, he will be motivated to respond in such a way that plays up to that friendship in requesting time to work out a solution.

But that isn't what you want, so you don't mail that letter. Going on to a second draft, you realize that your first draft contained some information that must be deleted:

- Phil knows that you have been friends for a long time. Reminding him of that serves no purpose here and does not help to meet your objective. If anything, mentioning your friendship will get in the way of your goals.

- Even if it is true, there is no point in saying that drastic action will be taken only as a last resort. Do you want Phil to believe that your primary objective is to avoid taking drastic action? If so, leave it in. But if you want him to think that your overriding goal is to increase sales, do not imply that drastic action will be taken as a last resort.

- *Please* and *as quickly as possible* are terms applicable to polite requests, not to urgent demands. Be specific about what you want and when you want it.

Taking those deletions into account and adopting a much tougher stance, your second draft becomes much more hard-hitting:

> Dear Phil:
>
> Sales in your territory are inexcusably low. Given the booming results we are seeing elsewhere and the successes of our competition in your region, I can conclude only that you are somehow doing something wrong.
>
> Whatever your problems may be, I expect you to correct them immediately. If we do not see a thirty-percent improvement in your sales by the end of the month, we will have no choice but to take drastic action. Specifically, if you can't do the job any longer, I'll find someone else who can!

That'll light a fire under Phil, but will it result in the increased sales you are after? Maybe it will; but then again maybe it will serve primarily to motivate him to concentrate on looking for another job rather than on improving your business. On what basis can you say that sales are "inexcusably" low or that Phil is doing "something" wrong? What is that "something"? There is no surer way to miscommunicate than telling people that they are doing something wrong and then not saying what that "something" is.

Another problem with the second draft is that ". . . if you can't do the job any longer. . . " implies that you think Phil is "over the hill." Combined with the vague accusations of fault, this personal affront will serve no purpose but to get Phil mad at you. Will that help? Being given only a few weeks to engineer a big boost in business, he may see no hope in continuing to work for someone who used to be on good terms with him, but who now is just another hardheaded boss.

So far, we've looked at one draft that used a twenty-year friendship as the motivational basis, and another draft that was based on personal attacks and the fear of being fired. For the third draft, let's leave out the friendship business, the accusations, the personal attacks, and the unreasonable demands. If you want to fire the guy, do it. But to expect a slumping business to turn around in only a few weeks is ridiculous, particularly when you don't even know *why* Phil's sales are slumping.

In this situation, your objectives should be to—

1. find out why sales are off in Phil's region;
2. take corrective action;
3. accomplish items 1 and 2 as quickly as possible;
4. make the best use of Phil's experience.

Each of these objectives is a portion of an overall goal: to increase business in the territory. Everything else—reinforcing your friendship, shaking Phil up or replacing him—are methods and means to an end, not targets. Here's the way the letter to Phil should look:

> Dear Phil:
>
> I am certain that you share my disappointment with the results shown in your latest sales reports. Something must be done to stem the recent tide of decreased bookings in your territory.
>
> Yours is the only region experiencing difficulties. Business is booming elsewhere and competition is doing well in all areas.
>
> By next Monday, let me know in writing precisely why your sales are significantly below par and what specific steps you are, or will be taking to turn your situation around. I will provide assistance and support to whatever extent is possible, but I cannot allow the current slowdown to be continued.

This draft may not by itself solve Phil's problems or yours, but it should be mailed. See what he says in his reply; you'll have it in only a few days. If the reply is unsatisfactory, you can always take a harder line next week. If, on the other hand, you see great business everyplace else and still feel compelled to solve Phil's problems before you know what those problems are, perhaps you should write to a psychiatrist who specializes in patients who panic easily.

What to say is always a question to be answered before writing, but what *not* to say is equally important. You cannot answer either question, however, unless you first ask yourself what knowledge the readers must have for your objectives to be met. Then, assess what the readers know or believe *before* reading what you have written. The *before* versus *after* difference represents the knowledge you must provide in writing. Nothing else is necessary, and nothing else should be added.

As you examine your drafts, look at *every* word, phrase, description, and statement, asking: "Does this help to meet my objectives? If not, why put it in?"

Sort everything into three categories:

1.   It helps; nothing here will hurt my chances.
2.   It may help, but it also may hurt.
3.   It hurts—readers will not react favorably.

Use only the material in the first category, or which can be rewritten to be moved into that category. In the early drafts of the letter to Phil, for example, category 2 information included the friendship reference, the business about taking drastic action only as a last resort, and the politeness with which the request for a response was made. In category 3 were the implications that Phil was at fault and past his prime, along with the unreasonable demands for quick results.

If it helps, use it. If it also may hurt, don't use it; rewrite so that it cannot hurt, or leave it out!

The Power of Doubt

Only one doubt is all it takes to scuttle communications. If it is strong enough in a reader's mind, a single negative reaction can be more powerful than an army of the most enticing incentives. The trick in communicating is to anticipate and eliminate negatives, or to minimize their importance as perceived by readers.

Nothing is perfect; no gains are achievable without cost, effort, or other form of expense; and no argument appeals to everyone. Accordingly, you'll have to go to another universe to find an absence of negatives. Even if you were to offer something for nothing, some people would react negatively, thinking that they want no part of schemes that are "too good to be true."

One could write an encyclopedia on different types of negatives, but let's think of them as being reader impressions of disbelief, distrust, disinterest, or inconsistency. Typically, negatives will occur whenever you—

1. provide information that conflicts with readers' beliefs without justifying the conflict or showing how it can be or has been resolved;

2. draw conclusions that readers find implausible or for any other reason in need of explanations you have not provided;

3. omit information or explanations without which readers might doubt, misinterpret, disagree with or not understand what you have said;

4. make what readers think is a mistake;

5. erroneously misinterpret and/or state readers' beliefs or wants;

6. contradict yourself without explaining why;

7. incorrectly assume that readers understand your jargon;

8. say something that readers will find offensive;

9. state what readers will see as unreasonable;

10. change the subject without telling why;

11. fail to clearly communicate specifically what you want, what you expect readers to do, and how, where, when, and why they should do it;

12. appear to your readers to be trying to motivate them to think or do something they perceive as being in conflict with their needs, objectives, or sense of right and wrong;

13. mistakenly assume that readers will draw the same conclusions you draw from a given amount of information;

14. provide explanations that are logical from your viewpoint, but not those of your readers;

15. offend your readers' intelligence or integrity;

16. back readers into a corner by suggesting that they have no alternative but to do something they consider to be contrary to their desires or best interests;

17. arrogantly assume that people will go along with you solely on the strength of your position, or your reputation;

18. write in a boring or pompous style;

19. neglect to provide an answer for the inevitable "What's in it for me?" question.

To a large extent, all negatives are unanswered questions of one form or another. Typical unanswered questions that can lead to negatives are:

So what?
Who cares?
What does this mean?
Why should I be interested in this?
Why is this information included here?
How did the writer reach this conclusion?
Doesn't this conflict with the previous paragraph?
Is this a fact or just someone's opinion?
Does this writer think I'm stupid or a mind reader?
What qualifies this writer?
What does this writer want me to do now?
Who does this guy think he is?
Are there any major risks inherent in this proposal?
What are they?
How likely are they to cause problems if I do what the writer wants?
Has anyone else done this before? With what results?
Why do I have to decide now? Why can't I think about this for a while?
What guarantees do I have of success?

In understanding your reasoning and the incentives you offer, readers may ask still more questions, including:

1. Why should I do that? (What's in it for me?)
2. On what basis is this valid?
3. Under which conditions will that happen?
4. On whose authority was this policy established?
5. With what ramifications can I proceed?
6. Where did that conclusion come from?

Even if your meaning is clear and your logic compelling, you can also trip yourself up by providing readers with opportunities to wonder, Isn't that date incorrect? Isn't this the opposite of what really happened? When did this fool escape from the asylum?

The questions posed so far are but a few examples of what an imaginative, inquisitive mind can dream up. No matter how well you answer the obvious questions, some readers will say to themselves "That's great, but what if. . . ." Ever watchful for proposals that do not cover all conceivable eventualities, such individuals are indeed hard to please.

The best way to deal with questions is to make certain that they are never raised. You do that by making no mistakes, by writing from the reader's viewpoint, by offering trust and hope, by sidestepping negatives, and by diverting reader thinking to every positive you can dream up.

Sidestepping

Just as incentives are what you offer to readers, criteria are the standards against which they measure whether your ideas are acceptable or unacceptable. Every such measurement is a decision made on the basis of comparing criteria with incentives. If you meet a particular standard, you get a positive reaction; otherwise, you get a negative. You win only when the positives outweigh the negatives. And that means in terms of importance, not merely in numbers. A big enough negative—perceived by a reader to constitute an unacceptable risk—can shift the balance against an army of positives not seen to be worth that risk.

Every decision can be separated into several aspects, and every reader has several criteria on any subject. In purchasing an item, for example, some people buy on price alone, while others look for style, and still others respond to factors such as durability, performance guarantees, or supplier reputation.

So what do you do when you're trying to "sell" your ideas in writing? You may think you are offering the greatest concept since the invention of the wheel, but chances are that what you've got has some pluses and some minuses as would be perceived by readers . . . *if* they had sufficient information.

But they *don't* have sufficient information! Before reading your first word, people may have some familiarity with you and your message, and they may even have some preconceived beliefs about the strengths and weaknesses of what you want them to do or think. But they do not have the whole story at that point; that's why you're writing—to tell them what they don't know.

That does not mean volunteering a totality of knowledge on every aspect of the topic you are discussing. Unless your objective is to publish an encyclopedia, it means meting out just enough information to ensure that you achieve a positive reaction on all fronts, and saying no more.

Take a close look at what your readers know about you and your ideas now—before you have written anything. Do they know nothing? Great! How are they going to find out about the fantastic incentives you are offering?

By reading what you will write.

Who then has total control over what readers will or will not be told? Who has absolute power to prevent them from forming negative reactions? Who has to take the blame if they don't like what you say?

You do.

Prior to putting any words on paper, ask yourself what criteria your readers will apply to judging your message. In other words, ask yourself what your readers want and whether you can give it to them. Do not, however, make the mistake of anticipating reader criteria on an overall basis; when people like or dislike something, they do so for specific reasons. Think ahead and make a list of what those reasons might be. In each case, ask yourself what would or would not appeal to readers and why.

When you're finished, you will have a list of strengths and weaknesses. Invariably, you will anticipate that your message can be extremely acceptable on some points, barely possible on others, and unacceptable on still others.

Examine what you have in the latter category. If a point is likely to be unacceptable, you may be able to sidestep a negative reaction by being less than complete in describing that point. Accordingly, "Having won the 1962 London Design Competition, we are an internationally recognized leader in graphic arts," is perhaps a true statement—one to be proud of. But it also needlessly raises questions that might lead readers to wonder what has happened since 1962, and whether the writer's creative juices have dried up since then. Why chance it? Leave the date out, and the sentence is still truthful, yet completely positive: "Having won the London Design Competition, we are an internationally recognized leader in graphic arts."

Now, the statement infers that the writer's current international reputation is due to winning the award in London, an act that would not be surmised to have taken place in the Dark Ages.

Dates are not the only type of information that should not be volunteered without good purpose. A sentence such as, "I worked closely for a couple of days with Mr. Armarc on the billion-dollar Webster dam project some years ago," shows familiarity with a person and a project, but the relationships are not strong. With a little editing, however, a much more powerful impression can be made: "I worked closely with Mr. Armarc on the billion-dollar Webster dam project."

A lie? No way! It's merely a good example of sidestepping a negative reaction.

Circumventing

Circumventing is sidestepping that detours our thinking toward specific implications. Who would want to interview a job applicant who has no degree? Someone who reads, "After four years at UCLA, I went directly into public accounting where I have specialized in corporate taxes for the past five years."

The implications here are that the four years at UCLA were continuous, on a full-time basis, and resulted in an accounting degree. None of that is stated, but it sure will be inferred.

Circumventing is what advertisers do when they think we may consider their goods or services to be overpriced. They divert our attention away from the cost by inundating us with a blizzard of incentives and asking us to call, write or visit for additional information and prices. Alternatively, they might have reason to believe that we will perceive their offering as having second-rate style or quality, in which case they would try to dazzle us with a low price.

Another way to circumvent potential negatives is to bury side-stepped material within the midst of other information.

> We offer a full range of surgical needles and accessories. Founded in 1880, our company has always been located in suburban Monsey, where we last month dedicated a new twenty-million-dollar needle research facility staffed with more than seventy doctors, scientists, and technicians.

This is typical of what might be written by a firm that has been in the surgical needle business for years.

Or, they may have just gotten into that business a month ago when the new facility opened. Since 1880, they have been making pile drivers, but now they want to (pardon the expression) penetrate the needle market. Concerned that the typical customer would be reluctant to buy from people who have no track record in surgical products, they could be circumventing their lack of experience by sidestepping a discussion of what they have been doing for the last century. The net result is an implication that the company is quite experienced in needles. Unless they knew otherwise, readers would not infer otherwise.

Notice that most of the words in this example are directed toward offering incentives: a full range of needles and accessories, a large financial commitment in a modern facility, and a capable staff. Taken together, these add up to an implication of being able to provide anything customers want in the needle arena. Within all that, "Founded in 1880. . . ." implies experience and reliability, while circumventing the newness of the company's entry into that arena.

OK, so you are not trying to write sales copy. Is your problem convincing a conservative boss to allocate funds for a new type of production machine instead of fixing the one you have now? In a report you could circumvent objections to a large capital outlay by saying in part:

> Stewart Manufacturing's new machine will double the production rate we would get if our existing equipment is upgraded. It will also enable us to operate on a two-shift basis with half as many personnel. As a result, the sixty-two hundred dollar machine will pay for itself in only three months; at the end of one year, our *net savings will exceed twenty thousand dollars*, including the repair costs we would not incur on the Jenkins machine we are using now.
>
> Those repairs, by the way, carry only a ninety-day warranty, so even if we were to stay with the Jenkins, we could in the near future again be confronted with the same decision before us now.
>
> Stewart has an excellent reputation and has been highly recommended by both Smith Industries and by our own Turbodigit division. They will provide us with extensive operator training and manuals.
>
> In light of the foregoing, your approval is requested to purchase the Stewart machine as quickly as possible.

Here, the boss is left with the implication that the only logical course of action would be to purchase the new machine.

The cost of that machine is divulged, but also circumvented, since it is unemphasized and buried in the middle of a long paragraph outlining incentives. Notice also that savings in one year will more than triple the initial cost. Rather than forcing the reader to dwell on the negative (cost), the paragraph uses underlining to divert attention to the good news (the savings).

Then comes the matter of warranties. By implication, the second paragraph suggests that repairing the old machine is likely to only delay replacing it. But how about the Stewart warranty? That's circumvented simply by not being mentioned. Perhaps the new machine has a warranty no longer than the one that comes with repairing the old machine.

The third paragraph is even sneakier. What if the Stewart machine is so new that no one else has bought one yet? Do you stress that fact, or do you sidestep and, as was done here, imply product reliability and reputation by showing that the *manufacturer* is well liked by others?

Sidestepping is not done anticipating that readers are stupid or blind; people will see prices no matter how deep they are buried, and they will eventually ask about cost before they buy. Employers will ask about experience, and people who hold purse strings will look for all kinds of reasons to spend nothing. The question is whether they will dwell on negatives or on positives, and whether they will be "turned off" at the outset or willingly move on to the next step in their decision process.

Sidetracking

You say you'd rather not discuss something? Change the subject. In addition to sidestepping, attention can sometimes be diverted from one topic by going on to something else that feeds the reader's ego. "For someone in your position, image is important. With the wardrobe I've suggested, you will look like a million dollars."

The style conscious among us would be very interested in looking as if they had a million dollars as long as they didn't have to spend that much to do so. Examining the sentence clinically, image is important for everyone, not just for those in certain positions, yet ploys like this do set the stage for making motivation easier.

Compliments are a great way to get a reader's ego working for you, as with:

> Frankly, we don't think we can afford to work with any but the best fund-raiser available. That's why we thought of you, particularly when you were recommended by six of our major benefactors.

What's "in it" for this reader to respond? Nothing, except to uphold a reputation and to meet his instinctive needs to do good, feel valuable and be praised. Combined with other information of a convincing nature, this little bit of sidetracking, as corny as it might seem, may do the trick.

Another way to sidetrack someone's thinking is to veer off into another area to delay action. This technique would be useful when someone is pressing you for a response and all you want is time. Accordingly, you could say:

> I'll find all the information you have requested, but first you must send to me a more detailed request including the date and title of each entry you want.

What do you do when those details are sent to you? Whatever you want—you didn't say that you would give any information to the reader; you said only that you would *find* it.

To sidetrack for *getting* information, act as if you are interested in doing something the reader might want you to do. Not in agreement with a client? A good way to improve communications may be to make it clear that you know who is in charge:

> You are of course the only person who can determine the approach that will do you the most good. Be assured that we will therefore follow your wishes to the letter.

> We will be in a much better position to serve your needs, however, if you would provide us with a more detailed summary outlining why the program has been changed and what your specific objectives are at this time.

Readers are not stupid, and endlessly gushing praise or fawning over them will not make points. But if you can sidetrack their thinking from confrontation or disagreement to a state more conducive to being motivated, you'll be that much further ahead.

Alternatives

Every attempt at communication is a matter of convincing readers to accept your ideas as opposed to other choices at their disposal. Readers *always* have other choices. You may be competing against someone else, or against factors such as prejudice, indifference, ignorance, fear, or other factors you might never anticipate unless you are a mind reader.

If nine tenths of your words say what is not good about other ideas, only one tenth is left to say what *is* good about your ideas. You may under such conditions convince readers not to go along with someone else, but that does not necessarily mean that they will go along with you. If unbeknownst to you, a new competitor arrives on the scene, you may lose out because you were more successful at defeating one approach than you were at promoting your own, while offering no argument against the guy who slithered in without your prior knowledge.

An occasional reference to someone else's weaknesses may not hurt your chances, but the bulk of your argument must be devoted to blowing your horn in a positive manner. Rather than saying, "Compared to our products, the competition has forty-percent lower fuel economy, half the room for service access, and only one third as many operator safety checks," and talking about what the other guy does not have, be positive. "We have forty percent higher fuel economy, twice the room for service access, and three times the number of operator safety checks." Boldly proclaim what you *do* have.

In a similar vein, "We will not have our meeting in New York this year," is by itself negative and open-ended, whereas a positive statement such as, "We will have our meeting in San Diego this year," is definite, specific, and significantly more powerful.

People have but a part of a story when a writer says only what will not be, what something does not have, or what they should not do. By saying what *will* be, what something *does* have, and what readers *should* do, however, a message is more complete, more specific, and therefore more meaningful and powerful.

Go Directly to the Bottom Line

Writing with power means requiring a reader to do an absolute minimum of thinking to understand your message, to pick up on your implications, or to conclude that your ideas should be accepted. Accordingly, what you say must lead directly to your "bottom line"—the most basic essence of your message, including all relevant explanations and justifications.

The bottom line is reached when readers have little or no need to think about, ask or answer questions such as:

> What's in it for me?
> What does this mean?
> On what basis is this valid?
> Why is this information included here?
> How did the writer reach this conclusion?
> So what?

The best way to prevent those questions from being asked is to give readers a direct route to the answers. As an example, "The calculations were corroborated by computer and by three different independent designers," is a nice little sentence that implies the simple belief that the calculations are correct. But why imply? Unless doing so will generate negatives, state that belief: "The calculations are correct." But that way, it could be seen as nothing more than an unjustified opinion. To go to the bottom line, justify that statement and the point is much more penetrating: "The calculations are correct; they have been corroborated by computer and by three independent designers."

Another sentence that fails to go to the bottom line is, "Removing the luggage rack will decrease your car's wind resistance."

That's nice, but so what? Is lower wind resistance a benefit unto itself, or is it merely a way to get a "bottom line" benefit that the sentence does not express? Less wind resistance means more efficient aerodynamics, but, "Removing the luggage rack will improve your car's aerodynamic efficiency," doesn't get to the bottom line either. More efficient aerodynamics means being able to go faster and to get better gas mileage. Accordingly, one might say, "By removing the luggage rack, your car will be able to go faster and to get better gas mileage." But that still runs the risk of posing a negative in the minds of readers who may ask, "On what basis does luggage rack removal result in better speed and mileage?"

So "head them off at the pass" and don't allow that question to be asked. Go directly to the bottom line and say:

> Removing the luggage rack will increase your car's aero-
> dynamic efficiency. Rather than using fuel and engine power to
> overcome wind resistance, you will therefore be able to achieve
> higher speeds and better gas mileage.

Theoretically, higher speed means an ability to travel faster from one place to another. Also, better gas mileage means saving money. But unless you are writing to young children or to people from Mars, these refinements are unnecessary; going to the bottom line does not mean treating readers as if they are idiots.

Many advertisers and politicians operate on the assumption that just about anything will eventually be believed if it is said often enough and boldly enough. Accordingly, we find ourselves bombarded with messages that say, in part, something like, "These sunglasses transmit only 0.05 percent of the ultraviolet and infrared light."

What does that mean? That you can't see anything through those glasses? What is the importance of transmitting such a small portion of specific kinds of light?

When they stop to think about it, most adults will realize that the purpose of sunglasses is to protect one's eyes from harmful light rays and that no one would be so impractical as to use sunglasses so dark that normal vision would be impaired. But the point is that they *do* have to "stop to think about it," to get that meaning from the sentence as written. And that isn't the only meaning they could derive; they might infer that the glasses have special purpose lenses too dark for normal use.

With a great deal of repetitive advertising including visual images, such inferences would not be a problem. But to effectively make your point in a single document, you have to be more direct:

> To protect our eyes from harmful radiation, these sunglasses
> transmit only 0.05 percent of the sun's ultraviolet and infrared
> light while allowing us to see normally during daylight hours.

Here's a case in which a sentence is vague because of a needless reliance on implications: "This calculation will give you unmatched accuracy in predicting economic trends."

Unmatched? Does that mean everything else is less accurate or that everything else is more accurate? "Unmatched" may be fine as an advertising ploy for writers who have nothing concrete to say, since most readers will infer *unmatched* to mean all others to be worse. If you do have a legitimate claim to make, however, make it directly at the bottom line: "This is the most accurate calculation you can get for predicting economic trends."

Government people, scientists, mathematicians, and engineers are notorious for using jargon, expressions, and notations that completely avoid the bottom line by being meaningless to most of the human race.

"After I get back from USMC headquarters, I'll call on the local FHWA offices. This means that Jane will have to contact UMTA and FHA people by herself," is a prime example of governmentese. Did you know that USMC stands for *United States Marine Corps*? That the FHWA is the *Federal Highway Administration*? If not, then you may not know that the UMTA is the Urban Mass Transportation Authority and that the FHA is the Federal Housing Administration. And if you knew what none of those things meant, you certainly did not know what the sentence meant.

Unless their purpose is to impress us with their knowledge of "in" terminology, writers are foolish to use undefined terminology. At the least, all such expressions should be fully defined with their first usage in a document: "I'll be at DOT (Department of Transportation) headquarters on Friday afternoon."

After that, the abbreviated form can be used as many times as necessary without confusing anyone.

Notice that going to the bottom line often means avoiding implications and explicitly expressing information in a direct, openly stated manner. In this regard, implications should be used primarily in two situations: when sidestepping negatives, and when hard-sell convincing is likely to be more difficult than allowing people to form their own conclusions.

The best way to motivate—explicitly or implicitly—is to go to the bottom line and to give readers that to which they will respond with the least amount of thinking, and the least likelihood of questioning your logic or your facts.

Be as Specific as You Can

Every time you mention a someone or a something, readers may form negative reactions unless you tell them—

> which one it is;
> what kind it is;
> how many there are;
> whose it is;
> how much is involved;
> what are its significant characteristics.

Then, for every description, activity, occurrence, or condition you mention, readers can be expected to want information such as:

> How did that happen?
> Why did that happen?
> To, from, or for whom is this being done?
> To, in, or from which direction or location?
> After, during, at, or before which time period?
> To what extent?
> With what regularity?

Not only do readers want this information, they want it in terms that they will perceive as being precise. A writer who is vague or ambiguous is likely to be seen as not being well informed, as having something to hide, or as not having a strong argument.

Statements such as, "We had very little money," are therefore weak compared to the more powerful and specific, "We had only three dollars."

In their enthusiasm to imply, some writers detour so far from their bottom line that they wind up with empty sentences such as, "We stand out in our field because of our in-depth approach to meeting your office supply needs," which comes across as mere advertising hype that says a grand total of nothing. What do *stand out* and *in-depth* mean? How does the writer know what your office supply needs are? Does the writer meet *all* office supply needs, or just those in certain areas? Which areas?

If you want to say something, say it!

> Compared to any other firm in the typewriter, stationery, and desk accessory supply business, we have more locations, more salespeople, a more complete catalog, more delivery trucks, and a wider range of products in stock for immediate delivery.

Spell it out. When you ask readers to swallow vague generalities like, "This is the largest firm of its kind in the world," you force them to ask what *of its kind* means. Is it the largest firm dealing in specific products or services? The biggest to do business according to some management philosophy? Or simply the largest to be headed up by someone with the same last name as that of their chief executive?

To answer those questions before they are asked, be specific: "This is the world's largest manufacturer of pet collars."

A little uneasy about making such an absolute declaration? That's fine—go to the bottom line as positively as you can: "According to our records, this is the world's largest manufacturer of pet collars."

Being specific means leaving no question as to your meaning. Saying, "You must pay us by Monday," for example, does *not* go to the bottom line. Does the sentence mean that the bill must be mailed by Monday, or does it mean that the payment must be received by Monday? Also, where must the bill be paid or received?

"Your payment must be mailed to our Chicago offices and postmarked no later than Monday" does not mean the same as, "Your payment must be received in our New York offices by Monday," which may not mean the same as, "Your payment must be received in our corporate offices by Monday."

The last three examples are all specific. Whereas the original version conveyed confusion, either of the three will communicate a specific message as long as one uses a letterhead that identifies the right mailing address.

To do what you want them to do, the way you want them to do it, readers must know *what*, *when*, and *where* you have in mind, *how* it should be done, and *who* is involved. To be motivated, they also must know *why*. If you are vague, the result may be confusion, negatives, or both. The more specific you are, however, the better your chances are of success.

Volunteering

Do not be so specific that you volunteer negatives. Leave volunteering to those who are heroes in adventure novels or war movies. Provide readers with no information or opinions that have even the slightest chance of evoking negatives. This means limiting the information you provide to that without which readers would not understand or accept your ideas.

Suppose for the moment that you are concerned that volunteering certain information might result in a negative reaction. Unless a reader has specifically asked for that information, however, you can leave that information out.

Put yourself in the shoes of a job applicant with thirty-years' experience as an electronics engineer, despite having graduated in 1948, with a degree in mechanical engineering. You see a help wanted ad that calls for an electronics engineer with ten-years' experience. The ad says nothing else about the employer's criteria, so you feel good about your chances. You apply in writing, opening with:

> Gentlemen:
> A 1948 mechanical engineering graduate of Rutgers University, I have. . . .

Congratulations! You have just "blown yourself out of the water." By being specific about your degree and year of graduation, you have created a first impression that positions you as being someone who not only is within a few years of retirement, but who also has what seems to be the wrong educational background. Did you say that the next twenty sentences illustrate your electronics expertise? That's terrific—the employer may read those sentences the next time he rummages through his wastebasket!

A more powerful approach would be to not volunteer the

damaging specifics, to sidestep on your length of experience, and to open the letter with:

> Gentlemen:
> An engineering graduate of Rutgers University, I have more than ten years' experience in electronics engineering.

Whenever you find yourself providing details, ask yourself whether they are really necessary and whether leaving them out or putting them in would be more beneficial to meeting your objectives. A sentence in a proposal, for example, might say that, "This design is identical to one we supplied last year to Harrison Industries, who used it in the production of pencils in their factory in Brazil."

But is the reader interested in pencil production? Will a similar design impress someone who is responsible for a radar factory in California? Or will the reader see negatives, perceive the design as being inapplicable and reject the design completely? Unless details help, don't volunteer them: "This design is identical to one we supplied last year to Harrison Industries."

If you must supply details about the Harrison job, focus on positives, even if the best you can do is, "This design is identical to one we successfully supplied last year to Harrison Industries."

Literally, this version says the supply itself was successful, while saying nothing about the use or application. By implication, however, those factors will be taken to have been successful as well.

Big numbers are impressive, but they must also be plausible and useful. "We shipped 151,217 tons of ore last year," sounds great, but, "My brother has watched 47,536 television programs since 1953," sounds like a fabricated number. Who would keep such statistics? Would the statement have any less impact if the count were only 47,535? Would the writer be more likely to make his point if the number were 47,537?

Rather than invoking those questions, a better way to go would be, "My brother has watched nearly 50,000 television programs since 1953."

But to sidestep the negatives that might arise in the minds of people who would question such a high number, an even better tact would be to say, "My brother has watched thousands of television programs since 1953."

One last reason for not providing details is that the reader may not want them and may be confused by their presence.

> David is an engineer I first met on June 22, 1968, when I went to Cincinnati for a job interview on my way back from a business trip that took me to San Francisco, Chicago, and Pittsburgh.

Presuming that the sentence is to convince the reader that you have known David for many years, the details of the business trip are unnecessary, as are the exact date and month of your first meeting. Depending on the impression you want to leave, you'd be better off saying something like, "David is an engineer I first met in 1968," or "David is an engineer I've known since 1968," or "David is an engineer I've known for more than fifteen years."

And if the reader already knows that David is an engineer, you can say, "I've known David for fifteen years."

Commit Yourself

Qualifiers are words that limit (or impose conditions on) the meaning of other words. A statement such as, "You can retire tomorrow" conveys information as if it were unconditional, but that's quite different from saying, "If you win the million-dollar lottery today, you can retire tomorrow."

Now, "You can retire tomorrow" is made conditional on winning the lottery, so the qualifier clause, "If you win the million-dollar lottery today" is essential to the meaning of the sentence.

But all qualifiers are not essential. Someone who writes, "Jack is perhaps the best salesman in our company," is not communicating. Such a sentence is obviously an opinion as stated, but what does the *perhaps* mean. That Jack is good but that someone else may be better? Who is that someone else? Why might he be better than Jack?

Or does *perhaps* mean simply that the writer is admitting to speaking from impressions rather than from an exhaustive examination of sales facts and figures? In that case, a more definitive approach would be to say, "Everything I know tells me that Jack is the best salesman in our company."

People with more confidence in their opinions, however, would be more prone to say, "Jack is the best salesman in our company" and leave it at that.

You're a fool to expect readers to accept your ideas if you communicate reservations about your facts, about your viewpoint, or about what you want. Qualifiers are a necessary part of describing and defining information, but if much of what you say straddles a fence of conditions, reservations, and limitations, you in essence will flash the yellow light of caution rather than the green light of GO! In this regard, "You may want to call him next Monday" is weak compared to, "You should call his office next Monday," which itself is weak when stacked up against, "Call him next Monday!"

Similarly, "In general, engineers are poor writers" is less emphatic than something like, "Many engineers are poor writers."

When people read a sentence such as, "I think that we will probably be successful," they get a double dose of "maybe" because *I think* denotes an opinion, and *probably* denotes something less than *definitely*.

One possible fix is, "I think that we will definitely be successful," but that is weak compared to, "I'm convinced that we will be successful," and that can be made more emphatic by saying, "We will definitely be successful," which can be made even more emphatic by rewriting to say, "We *will* be successful."

Alternatively, a wishy-washy statement such as, "I'm not certain, but I have a suspicion that what you want is at the research center in California" can be made more definite by saying that, "What you want can most likely be found at the research center in California."

Note also that, "We expect to finish the job by Thursday or Friday" is stronger when expressed as, "We will finish the job no later than Friday."

If you *must* express reservations, do so on a bottom line basis. Saying, "Alan will probably not graduate until June" is not going to the bottom line because the qualifier is not explained. To complete the picture, one would have to add more information:

> Alan will probably not graduate until June. He could graduate in January, but that would mean giving up his job to take additional courses this fall, and he cannot afford to lose the income.

As is the case with many other facets of writing, qualifier use must be evaluated on a case-by-case basis. The situation, and not some grammar professor, determines how definite you can be, how definite you must be, and how much has to be explained to make a point.

If your main purpose is to tell a reader that you are uncertain, express as many reservations as you like. To convince and motivate, however, be positive, be emphatic and, unless you want restaurant seating, don't think in terms of reservations.

6

TAILORING

When dealing with only one reader, effective communication is a matter of determining the beliefs, needs, emotions, and intelligence guiding that reader's thinking, and tailoring your writing accordingly. To motivate someone else, however, you must recognize that different people have different brains, different ways of thinking, and different ways of reacting to what they see in print. This means that each reader must, to the greatest extent practical, be treated as "one of a kind" who may not be motivated by the same argument or incentives that will work with any other reader.

The advertising and direct mail industries have developed sophisticated techniques for customizing written communications without having to attempt the obviously unworkable task of writing to each reader individually. As applied to letters, reports, and proposals, those techniques are described in this chapter.

Everything for Everybody

Some writers offer "everything for everybody" as they attempt to reach all imaginable points of view, in the hope that every reader will find at least some incentives of interest. A typical example is a job application letter that in part says:

> After ten years as a design engineer and engineering manager in the air-conditioning and jet engine industries, I moved into marketing management, where for five years I was responsible for merchandising and promoting machinery components,

sporting goods, consumer electronics accessories, and pharmaceutical instruments.

In 1978, I founded my own advertising business, which specialized in serving the needs of colleges and universities throughout the middle Atlantic states and New England. After four years, however, I sold that business to a large publisher.

Since then, I have worked for two New York City management consultants as a specialist in outplacement and executive recruitment for the banking industry.

No matter how much else the letter says elsewhere and no matter how much it provides in the way of examples illustrating this particular applicant's capabilities, it will get dismal results. This is because it communicates too many negatives:

1. Most employers believe that for any other than entry level jobs, the best applicants are specialists with at least five years' recent experience in a specific discipline.

2. Most employers believe that an applicant is more reliable if he is committed to a specific career direction. The writer, however, seems committed only to changing industries and work specialties on a regular basis.

3. Having worked for more than twenty years and having been self-employed, the writer will be perceived as someone who will not be satisfied with a low-level job or a low-level salary. The preference of most employers is to pay low-level salaries.

4. Since the applicant has sold a business, he may be perceived as someone who has money to fall back on if a job does not last long. Many employers, however, believe that maximum productivity comes from employees who cannot afford to lose their jobs.

5. Anyone who has been self-employed may be considered as a potential risk who may prefer the freedom of working for himself to the regimentation of reporting to a supervisor.

6. Someone in the petrochemical industry (or any other business not named in the letter) will be likely to say, "All this experience is impressive, but what does this applicant know about my business? What's in it for *me*?"

These negatives and unanswered questions are not imaginary, nor are they reprinted from magazine or newspaper articles; they were actually volunteered by the writer.

Imagine what would happen if the chairman of a corporation, in his annual report to stockholders, were to include the following paragraphs as background information on company activities:

A year ago, our president announced to you that shortly we would be introducing a new line of electronic tennis racquets. Unfortunately, he was mistaken; the product was not ready until eight months afterward.

Initially, the delay was caused by our sales manager and chief designer who resigned after a dispute with our board of directors on product introduction strategy. We replaced both executives within two months, but our market research consultant then advised us that our competition had just introduced a new product that was similar to what we were planning to offer.

As a result, we were forced to revamp our thinking and to initiate a new phase of development work to make certain that when we introduced our racquet, it was the best on the market. After two more months and fourteen interim designs that were not satisfactory, we were ready from a design standpoint; this was three months ago.

To be certain that the new design would meet with customer approval, we then commissioned a new market survey. The survey confirmed that our plans were on the right track. Accordingly, our official sales "launch" occurred four weeks ago.

I am happy to report that the results to date have been excellent. We have doubled our advertising budget to maximize promotion of the racquet's unique range-finding and spin control features, and sales have already exceeded projections to this point in time.

Perhaps electronic tennis racquets are not yet a reality, but the types of situations depicted in this report are not at all unreal. Even the most successful companies experience dissension, poor planning, lack of adequate market research, unforeseen delays, and failed development prototypes. Not all of those failings occur at once, and not all of them are so costly as to lead to financial ruin, but they do happen from time to time.

Assuming that the intent of a board chairman is to impress stockholders rather than to motivate them to sell their shares, however, you'll rarely see a company's problems aired in public.

Admittedly, reports such as the previous one, will impress readers who like candor. It may also go over well with anyone who likes companies that profit by persisting in the face of problems. But most readers will draw a different perception; they'll see a firm run by inept management that has been lucky in a recent product introduction that is succeeding in spite of an obvious lack of planning and control.

Everything means telling all there is to tell, which means expressing or implying both positives and negatives. Everything also means disaster, because no reader wants everything; each reader wants something different, and *every* reader wants only positives. Accordingly, "everything for everybody" usually means that each reader gets exposed to at least one negative. The net effect of such a message is the same as it would have been if the intent were to offer "negatives for everybody."

Something for Everybody

Modern technology notwithstanding, no one can write a sentence that is both understandable and interesting to readers at random. If most Americans were to read, *"Lorsque l'affichage cesse diettre visible on manque de contraste, la pile doct etra changee"* in the instructions for a calculator, most of them would not comprehend what was being said unless they were fluent in French. Accordingly, foreign manufacturers usually provide instructions in more than one language, a courtesy that allows us to see the statement in French also expressed as, "When the display is fainting or losing contrast, the battery should be replaced." In this way, the instructions have "something" for everybody.

In different formats, the same approach applies to many other types of communications, most notably business-to-business sales proposals. Proposals often must be read by several people, each of whom has a different concern in addition to being interested in the proposal as a whole.

To address each of those concerns, one could write a different proposal for each reader, but that would be doing things the hard way. An easier approach would be to subdivide the message into segments that address each area of significant reader concern. Primary headlines could be used to highlight each subdivision, and therefore to attract readers to subdivisions in which they have primary interest. At the same time, they could readily identify those subdivisions in which they had little or no interest.

In this way, a sales manager might study sections entitled REAL-ISTIC IMPACT ON SALES GROWTH and LONG-TERM BENE-FITS, while skimming through two sections on PRICES and TECHNICAL SPECIFICATIONS and perhaps reading none of the words under another called TERMS AND CONDITIONS. The chief engineer, on the other hand, would be more likely to focus on specifications and pay no attention to sales impact, whereas the controller could be expected to concentrate primarily on prices and terms and conditions.

Headlines are not always necessary (particularly in shorter proposals), but *something for everybody* is a commonly used technique for keeping multiple readers happy in one document. To make that technique work, however, one must be selective so that it offers *no negatives for anybody*.

Being Selective Keeps Everybody Happy

The difference between "everything for everybody" and "something for everybody" is obviously that *something* is less than *everything*. How much less is a function of both your objectives and your readers' needs. All you need is a clear, precise answer to, "What is the *minimum* information I have to divulge to accomplish my objective?" You will know just how selective you have to be.

A case in point is the job application letter shown on page 77.

The only reasonable objective of such a letter is to get an interview; no one ever gets hired unseen merely on the basis of a résumé or letter. To motivate people to take the time to interview you, however, you must first convince them that such time would be well spent.

But employers do *not* want to see that you have specialized in a field about which they know nothing, that you have often changed fields, employers, and industries; that your salary needs may be higher than they can afford; or that you may be an independent sort who would resist responding to orders from a demanding boss.

Employers want to see that what you offer is as similar as possible to their concept of perfection. In evaluating job-seekers, that concept invariably refers to one's job experience in a particular field as well as one's educational background.

Come in with characteristics similar to these, and you'll get an interview with anyone who has a current opening. Show a glaring lack of similarities, however, and you might as well be writing to Santa Claus. Can't show similarities in some areas? That's OK—completely sidestep those areas. Say nothing about them and focus only on your strengths.

No one letter or résumé can do that for all prospective employers. Using "cover" letters with printed résumés won't help either; cover letters can tailor by adding positives, but there's no way they can subtract negatives from what is already included in an "everything for everybody" résumé. The only effective thing to do is to tailor a separate letter to every potential employer.

Board chairmen cannot send correspondence to every stockholder, but tailoring principles still apply. The goal of a corporate report is usually to inform stockholders that the corporation is sound, well-run, profitable, and growing. This is the message that stockholders want to read, and it is also the message that prospective stockholders want to see before investing.

Will talking about problems build stockholder confidence? Will shareowners be pleased to find out that the competition's plans were totally unanticipated? Will the public be happy to see that market research was done *after* the product was already developed? How thrilled will they be to see that several interim designs failed during the design process or that the ad budget had to be doubled? Stockholders don't want to see any of that. If that's what you give them, they're the ones who will be selective—they'll put their money elsewhere.

What they want to see is that business is booming, or at least that things are looking up. Yes, they will always be happy to hear that past problems have been solved, but you can bet that they are not interested in knowing all the details about those problems. Compared to the letter shown on page 79: "We decided to conduct additional market research and to incorporate several design improvements before introducing our new electronic tennis racquet. That strategy has obviously paid off; although the product was introduced only a month ago, sales are already exceeding expectations," is harder-hitting because it tells readers only what they want to know.

Segmentation

Aside from recognizing that "something" is less than "everything," you must also realize that "everybody" is *never* the entire human race, but only those people who are going to read and have to make use of what you are writing.

Segmentation is the process of dividing readership into groups having similar interests, and writing a separate "something for everybody" letter, report, or proposal to each group. A group may have one person or a million people. As long as every group sees what it wants to see, however, segmenting will enable each to be as happy as possible.

When readers have a strong commonality of interests, as exemplified by stockholders looking for a profit, "everybody" consists primarily of five groups of people when the company's shares are publicly traded on a stock exchange:

1. current stockholders
2. potential (future) stockholders
3. stock analysts

4. stockbrokers

5. government agency types who monitor and regulate the way corporations report to stockholders

Groups 1 through 4 have many interests in common, while group 5 doesn't care whether the company thrives or goes bankrupt; their interests are restricted to the manner in which the company reports its finances and represents itself. For these five groups, saying "something for everybody" is simply a matter of addressing the needs of each group without saying anything that any other groups would find to be negative.

But things aren't that simple. There's a sixth group—the company's employees—that has somewhat different interests. Sure, all employees know that a profitable company is one that is best equipped to provide job security and pay raises, and to that extent all employees have a stake in helping their employer to make healthy profits. But what employees really want to know is how much of their employer's profits are going to trickle down to the work force—not in abstract terms, but in actions and hard cash. "These profits are great," says the typical worker, "but what's in it for me?"

Whether they should (or have a right to) feel like that may be debatable, but the fact is that they *do* feel like that, and the people who write annual reports must either recognize that fact or fail to communicate.

Too often, this does not happen. Annual reports are written for the benefit of telling the investment community what they want to read, and since most employees do not own shares in the companies for which they work, their viewpoints are not addressed. Let's face it; shareowners want profits to be expressed as dividends for people who own stock, not as salary increases and other employee benefits.

Satisfied employees will not get upset about the contents of an annual report, but they will when a company tells its stockholders that business is booming while at the same time freezing salaries and when there's rumors of impending layoffs.

As soon as readers perceive an inconsistency or lie, they get turned off—they will feel that their instinctive need to be safe is not being met, and they will lose trust in the writer. To a company, this can be disastrous when that happens to the shareowners *or* to the work force. Workers may stay with an employer to survive, but there's a big difference between an enthusiastic employee and one who exerts only the minimum effort necessary to avoid getting fired.

To avoid such situations, a wisely run company will go right to segmentation by writing separately to the work force and telling them what *they* want to hear: "Yes, we are now profitable, but unless we curb costs until we accumulate enough business to sustain us over the long haul, all of our jobs will be in jeopardy." By explaining to the bottom line (and by not saying the same thing every year as profits and executive salaries continue to grow), and by remembering to convey hope that the situation will be resolved in the near future, bad feelings can be avoided.

Or, say you wanted to form your own corporation that would someday be able to announce how rosy its future looks. A great goal, but first you will have to get some customers. But you don't merely start calling prospects at random or knocking on any doors you can find; you start by deciding who is most likely to want to use your services and why.

Assume that your intent is to sell and service computers and computer accessories. You know the business, you've worked with all kinds of computers, and you have programmed just about everything from desktop "personals" to the big "mainframes" used in business and scientific applications. In theory, every business and virtually every home is a potential customer.

The best way to promote yourself is through segmentation. The following are only a few of the reader groups you might contact with a well-written sales letter:

> home computer market for computer games, educational purposes, personal financial planning and record-keeping purposes, and word-processing applications
>
> record-keeping for self-employed individuals
>
> record-keeping, payroll, inventory control and word-processing applications for slightly larger companies

> large business markets corresponding to the small business markets just described
>
> record-keeping and word-processing purposes for the school market
>
> engineering and scientific markets for individuals, small and large businesses and schools

That's more than a dozen separate markets. In your neck of the woods, some of those markets may have thousands of readers, others only a handful. Write a different message to each. Tell the schools what you can do for schools, with equipment and programs tailored for, and customized to, the needs of schools. Do the same for each of the other markets. Tell each that you specialize in meeting their kinds of needs.

Don't tell them what you can do for others: "What's in it for me?" is *not* answered by pointing out what you can do for someone else.

Fill in the Blanks

Customizing materials for different readers is sometimes best accomplished by tailoring a basic document by simply changing a few key words. Selling computer services, for example, might be accomplished in part by using a sentence that said,

> The TURBODATA [1] computer, complete with [2] for only [3], has been used by thousands of [4] to meet their [5] needs.

Where some of the possible options would be:

1A.   Model 6
1B.   Model 7
1C.   Model 8
1D.   Model 9
1E.   Any other model number as appropriate

2A.   a letter-quality printer
2B.   an efficient printer

2C. built-in screen
2D. built-in screen and letter quality printer
2E. more than fifty games and a built-in screen

3A. ⎫
3B. ⎪ enter appropriate
3D. ⎬ cost here
3E. ⎭

4A. plumbers
4B. small business owners
4C. public school districts
4D. engineering consultants
4E. parents
4F. homeowners
4G. corporations

5A. record-keeping
5B. word-processing
5C. customer file
5D. order entry
5E. computational
5F. educational
5G. children's educational
5H. payroll
5I. inventory

Given even the relatively few options shown, the same sentence can say,

> The TURBODATA Model 9 computer, complete with a built-in screen for only $1,575, has been used by thousands of small business owners to meet their inventory and payroll needs,

or

> The TURBODATA Model 6 computer, complete with a letter quality printer for only $3,795, has been used by thousands of public school districts to meet their record-keeping, computational, educational, and word-processing needs.

Hundreds of other possibilities can be customized to suit any readership segment.

Filling in the blanks also works for people writing job application letters. That way a sentence such as, "A _____ of Rutgers University, I have more than _____ years' experience in _____," can be used to say, "A 1961 mechanical engineering graduate of Rutgers University, I have more than twenty-years' experience in the design and marketing of industrial noise control products and services."

Giving away the writer's age by indicating the year of graduation, the sentence also highlights specific job functions in one particular industry. This would be fine if there was a need for someone with that much experience in that particular industry.

For different readers, the same writer could, if applicable, fill in the blanks differently and with complete honesty say,

A graduate of Rutgers University, I have more than ten-years' experience in all phases of advertising design, copywriting, and placement.

The reader may be asked about age and degree, but that will occur later on, *after* the letter has accomplished its objective of making a good first impression. If that impression is good enough, the answers won't matter then.

Slant

When slanted in different directions, documents can motivate different readers to have different reactions. This means making conscious choices relative to whether and how to be optimistic or pessimistic, whether to focus on good news or bad news, how to sequence good news and bad news, and which aspects of a message to focus on.

Half empty or half full? An up view or a down view can be emphasized to suit any occasion. "If we fail to negotiate the loan, we will not be able to stay in business," for example, is a negative or pessimistic way of looking at things. A more positive slant would be, "This loan would enable us to prosper."

Which is best depends on who the readers are and what their viewpoints are. Writing to a friend who might be influential in getting you the loan, you would want to emphasize the gravity of the situation by stating the pessimistic view. To a bank president, however, you'd be better off to adopt the more optimistic stance, since banks don't like to deal with borrowers who are desperate.

Writers always have a choice of slants.

"If Dan hadn't solved our design problems, we would have lost the order; the customer loved Dan's ideas, however, and asked us to start production immediately," emphasizes Dan's role in overcoming problems that might have otherwise prevented closing an order. If the intent were to downplay Dan and to emphasize getting the order, a different slant would be to say: "We have the order. The customer loved Dan's ideas and asked us to start production immediately." Still another slant would be to not mention Dan at all and to focus entirely on the business aspects of what happened: "We have the order. The customer loved our ideas and asked us to start production immediately."

"All positives, no negatives" does not mean that bad news, problems, or pessimistic outlooks have to be swept under the rug. As shown in the last two examples, presenting a negative outlook can be a dramatic way to make a point. Taking a negative tact can also, however, add information you might not wish to convey. To someone who knows Dan but is unaware of what design problems he solved, for example, you may generate a negative reaction by not describing what those problems were. Someone who doesn't know Dan might also have a negative reaction if Dan were not identified in sufficient detail.

Different readers, different slants; all you have to do is to tailor to suit.

What Do You Want First? Good news or bad news? "Bad" news can to some readers be as disastrous as finding out that they can't get something for nothing and that they have to do something or pay something to avail themselves of those wonderful incentives you are offering. Under those circumstances, you must first make those incentives appear irresistible and then announce what readers have to do to accept your ideas. This is why sales offer letters usually highlight incentives and use a lot of space to emphasize benefits, while showing price last.

The opposite tact is taken when the price is so low that it can be used as an attractive attention-getter at the beginning. An example of such an opening is shown on page 101.

What comes first is *always* a matter of what will do the best job of attracting and keeping reader attention. If bad news will best rivet a reader's mind to your every word, put it up front, but if it will turn people off, save it for last.

Even if bad news is not emphasized, what comes first is often what readers assume is most important. In the example about Dan's contribution to a sale, the first version starts with a sentence referring to Dan's ability to overcome problems, whereas the second and third versions start out by saying that the company has the order. This shift in sequence leads directly to a shift in emphasis.

Tough Guy or Pussycat? You can be either, depending on which identity will do you the most good. Which identity that is depends on the reader; some people respond best when kicked in the teeth; others are more likely to be motivated when complimented.

If you do not know the reader and have no certain information as to his likely reaction to being prodded, pushed, forced or stroked, keep your personality in the background and represent yourself as an honest person who is offering an honest proposition based on valid information. Use implications and reader viewpoint logic to make your case and be certain to come across as being trustworthy.

If you know the readers well or have a good handle on how they will respond to different types of stimuli, tailor your writing accordingly. Some may be best motivated by telling them: "Check your work carefully. Regardless of the circumstances, errors cannot be tolerated. If you need assistance, call me. Otherwise, I shall expect the project to be completed on time, within budget, and without problems," whereas others might respond more favorably if they were told:

> I am confident that you can get this project done on time, within budget, and without errors or any other problems. If you need

any assistance, however, do not hesitate to call me; I will make myself available to lend a hand at any time.

Both versions are right only for the right reader. Have some of each? Segment accordingly.

One on One

No one likes to talk to a machine or a corporation, and none of us wants to be treated like a thing, or as one of the masses. We see ourselves as individuals and we like to be treated as individuals exchanging ideas with other individuals. We therefore respond best to material that gives the impression of having been written for our eyes only by one specific writer. Several techniques will help to create such an impression even if you are actually sending the same document to many different people.

Personalize the Package. At no time is "What's in it for me?" more important than the time when someone receives an envelope containing something you have written. Accordingly, your best bet is to insert first names, middle initials, and last names in business correspondence. And don't forget titles; some people are proud of their titles and if you slight their titles, you may slight them. Use nicknames only if you know the person well or if he has previously given you reason to believe that a particular nickname is acceptable.

Names are not always available when doing sales mailings, and in those instances titles alone can be used, but doing so is a distant second best; addressing someone by his title at an office is as impersonal as sending mail to "occupant" at a private residence. In your estimation, is "occupant" mail written specifically with *your* unique needs in mind?

Hardly. But when you get something with your name on it, you know that it is not for your boss, not for your neighbor, and not for the guy in the next office. You do, however, know that whatever's in that envelope *is* for you.

Computer address labels are a giveaway to a mass mailing.

Individually typed envelopes, on the other hand, look as if they were prepared specifically for the person. Labels are therefore seen as impersonal, while separately typed addresses imply that a writer has gone to some trouble to see that one specific reader gets one specific document.

With the right word-processing equipment, envelopes can be typed automatically by the thousands, but we can't tell the difference between them and those that are done individually. If it looks like it was prepared individually, readers will infer that an envelope *was* prepared individually, and they will therefore be more interested in the contents of that envelope.

Handwriting can also be used for addressing, but aside from being impractical for quantity correspondence, handwriting is generally inappropriate for business correspondence and is often illegible. Yes, handwritten addresses may in certain instances be effective attention-getters; they may also con some readers into believing that an envelope contains something from a personal friend, but handwriting can also backfire; some readers may not be able to read your handwriting, while others can be expected to look upon handwritten envelopes as being unprofessional and unlikely to contain material of importance.

Use Your Return Address Only When it Helps. The postal service needs your return address to get mail back to you in case it can't be delivered. But they don't need your name for that purpose.

Many writers, however, cannot resist putting their name atop their return address on an envelope; this is fine if a reader is waiting with the proverbial "bated breath" for mail from you. If the reader, however, perceives by seeing your name, that an envelope contains information which is not necessarily welcome, your name may work against you. Examples are envelopes that obviously contain bills, sales circulars, requests for donations, or eviction notices.

People are likely to read the contents of all envelopes in time, but why motivate them to wait? Unless identifying yourself will help, appeal to your reader's curiosity by using quality envelopes, individually addressed with your return address, but not your name. If you are classy enough, people will not be able to resist quickly looking within.

Personalize the Contents. For the same reason that you should have alternate ways of identifying yourself on envelopes, you should have different ways of presenting yourself on a letterhead. Something presented on business stationery is viewed as representative of the named company or organization, while those same ideas will be looked upon as strictly your own if the letterhead states only your name, home address, and home telephone number.

Personalize to the extent appropriate for your relationship with the reader and for the image you wish to create. If you are on a first name basis with the reader, use first names. Or, use a combination: "Mr. Robert J. Marks" can be used to address a letter that has "Dear Bob" as the salutation. That same letter can have "Sandra Green" typed below a signature that says "Sandra" or "Sandy."

Another way to personalize when signing off is to say "Best regards" or "Best personal regards" instead of the more traditional and stuffier "Very truly yours."

The text of a document can be personalized by incorporating the reader's name into the opening sentence of a paragraph, as in "We are pleased, Mr. Stewart, to award you our merit of excellence for on-time delivery during the past twelve months." Even if you give the same award to fifty others, Mr. Stewart will infer that you have singled him out for his accomplishments.

As with envelopes, contents should be individually typed, or at least look individually typed. Printing may be fine for flyers and sales brochures, and photocopying may be OK for inter-office memos with wide distribution, but if you want to make someone think that you have gone to a lot of trouble to communicate a personalized message, type it out or use a word processor.

You and I. One-on-one written communications begin with the writer being *I* or *me*, but when someone writes and signs a letter on behalf of a company or an organization, *we* can be used to create and reinforce the image of the writer being backed up by others rather than speaking as an individual.

Then, there are documents that are not signed by a person, but sent from companies, groups, or organizations talking as *we*. Upon seeing such documents, recipients have no knowledge of writer identity and no knowledge of whether one or several writers were involved.

In either case, the reader must always be treated as an individual *you* and not as part of some larger body of people. Rather than saying, "Our promotional programs can generate sales for your company," personalize by saying, "Our promotional programs can generate sales for you." Better yet, go right to the bottom line and say, "Our promotional programs can make money for you," which is more direct and therefore more personalized than, "Our promotional programs can make money for your company." Similarly, "I can help your people to prevent age discrimination," tells the reader that you consider him or her to be part of a crowd rather than an individual. A better statement would be, "I can help you to prevent age discrimination."

Also, focus on what the reader will get rather than on what you will give. Instead of saying that, "We will give you an unconditional guarantee of satisfaction," you would be better off saying, "You will get an unconditional guarantee of satisfaction."

Use of "I" is fine for personalizing your opinions, your accomplishments, and your hopes, but do not bury readers in a sea of expressions such as "I did this," "I believe that," and "I want something else." Too many I's may make you look too egocentric to suit some readers, but you can usually avoid such problems by rewording. "I prefer the beige wallpaper," for example, can be changed to, "My preference is beige." Or, it can be made even more emphatic as, "The beige looks best."

Be on the Same Side as the Reader. Aside from meaning writer plus someone else, *we* can also mean writer plus reader, thinking and acting together to battle some common enemy, to tackle some common problem or simply to do something in unison.

Being on the same side means going after the same goals relative to the particular matter about which you are writing. That way, you can position yourself as the "cavalry" coming to the reader's rescue, as in:

> Our taxes have risen too fast in recent years. Working together as a team, however, we can reduce government expenses and cut real estate expenses.

Even when using *I*, the togetherness approach may be useful in building trust: "I want to help. We can lick this problem."

Instead of heaping a problem on a reader with a statement such as, "You are going to have to do something quickly," you can work together with the reader to share the load: "We are going to have to do something quickly."

When one writer encounters resistance, another in the same organization may be able to be successful by promoting togetherness:

> I apologize for the insensitive way in which our people have been handling your claim to this point. We can undoubtedly come to a mutually acceptable agreement, however, by adopting the following procedure: . . .

Don't Blame the Reader. A reader may be totally wrong and completely at fault, but you'll only create resistance by saying so in so many words. Instead of saying, "You miscalculated the costs by 52 percent," and attributing blame to the reader, the same information can be provided in a less offensive manner by saying, "The costs were miscalculated by 52 percent" and not personalizing negatives.

Alternatively, shift the blame to someone else. Instead of saying, "You are mistaken," fewer feathers will be ruffled if you can shift blame by saying, "Someone has given you the wrong information."

Stubborn readers, when combined with stubborn writers, add up to an impasse in which all arguments boil down to "I'm right, you're wrong," rather than, "Here's how we can both benefit." Don't fall into that trap; if all you do is to prove the other guy wrong, you will not necessarily succeed in convincing him that you are right. A statement such as: "Your expense figures are obviously incorrect. You state fixed costs as being 10 percent of sales, but every year for the past 5 years, our costs have not exceeded 6 percent of sales," is more likely to lead to inflamed tempers than to transferred ideas. A more productive tact would be to throw the reader off guard by acknowledging where he is right and, if possible, by admitting some minor error you have made. Then, instead of stating that the reader has erred, asking for further explanation, as in:

> Your annuity figures are of course correct, and your tax estimates, my analysts tell me, are more indicative of probable

revenue trends than were those I included in my letter to you of November 10. On the matter of expenses, however, note page 16 of our annual report; the past 5 years have shown costs to be no more than 6 percent of sales. Could you explain why projections show 10-percent expense estimates?

Give Credit Where Credit Is Due. Or maybe where it is not due. Can you on purpose misconstrue what a reader meant in previous correspondence? Compliment the reader for agreeing with you. This is the old trick of allowing a reader to believe that your ideas are actually his. People may have a more difficult time of disagreeing with themselves than with you. Instead of arguing and pleading by saying: "If, as you claim, we cannot get financing for a new building, can we get any assistance in securing federal grants for program expansion? There must be something you can do for us!" you may be better able to get the reader on your side by saying:

Your letter of July 17 gave me a great idea. As you have pointed out, we have no way to finance a new building, so the only other solution is to use the bank's influence to capitalize on federal grants for program expansion. I'll call you later this week to start working with you on grant applications. Thanks for the inspiration.

Not all tailoring techniques are applicable to every situation, but every document is a prime candidate to some form of tailoring, whether it be to the situation, to the group to whom you are writing, or to the peculiarities of but one difficult reader.

Tailoring is no big deal; it is merely remembering that you are communicating with one person at a time and that each person thinks as a unique entity with unique needs that can be met only with unique approaches. Address that uniqueness and you'll be moving in the right direction. Ignore it and you're asking for failure.

7

READABILITY

You may have a truckload of reasons for seeing to it that your words are read, but those reasons must be communicated. Your first priority is therefore to get and keep a reader's attention and interest. This means writing in such a way that readers feel compelled to start reading and to not stop until they finish. Accordingly, whatever you write must be easy to identify as containing information of interest, easy to read, easy to follow and understand, and interesting to read and not boring or repetitive.

Rather than straining to discover your meanings, readers should have no trouble identifying what you are talking about, your arguments and logic, what you offer as incentives, and what you want them to do or think.

Before a document can motivate people to accept your ideas, it must motivate them to read those ideas. People won't read something just because you send it to them; they'll read only if it has readability—if it obviously covers a topic of interest to them and if they believe that they can quickly and easily find out what it says.

Readability provides you with the means for emphasizing the strengths of your argument so that they stand out and cannot be missed. Contrary to popular belief, however, strengths do *not* speak for themselves and they do *not* stand out of their own doing. That's up to you and that's what this chapter is all about.

One Subject at a Time

Motivation in print is best accomplished when you have a reader's undivided attention. In most business situations, however, readers are constantly faced with distractions and interruptions over which neither they nor you have control.

Why add to all that by veering off into topics that divert a reader's concentration away from the subject you want emphasized? Unless your writing has a clear focus, readers may be motivated to stop and wonder why you have begun discussing topics that do not relate to the rest of what you have said.

Written materials need not necessarily have a narrow scope, but all topics in a document must be directly related to one another. If diverse subjects are covered, they must have some common basis that binds them together in such a way that the reader can see how they relate and why they are mentioned. Otherwise, they have no business being there.

So pick your track and stay in it from beginning to end by focusing on one subject or subject grouping. Do not write about anything else unless you can show strong and direct relationships in ways such as:

- cause and effect
- chronological sequence in a chain of events
- one subject being a well-defined aspect of another
- commonality or similarity in areas such as age, function, style, size, derivation, background, capabilities, ownership, or position
- one subject illustrating or explaining the other

Even if multiple topics can be dealt with collectively without confusion, grouping is not advisable if one subject in your opinion must be given primary emphasis. Rather than forcing such a subject to compete for a reader's attention, give it a document all its own and write about the other subjects elsewhere.

Go Right for the Jugular

People do not necessarily read everything they get, and they don't always finish everything they start to read. In a typical business environment, so much is going on simultaneously that unless you are able to command and keep a reader's attention from the outset, some of what you write may not be read, and that which is read may not be read carefully. Motivation must therefore begin with word one. Open aggressively in a way that will compel readers to want to start reading your letter, report, or proposal *now*, without the slightest hesitation.

One way to do this is with an attractive title. Perhaps we cannot "tell" a book by its cover, but publishers have known for years that they *can* sell a book by its title, particularly if that title is intriguing and generates curiosity. If readers are interested in the subject matter and if the title suggests that what follows contains information not previously known, they will start reading because the title will imply a strong message: "Here's a way to find out something new about a topic that interests you!"

Accordingly, titles are more than names for identifying the subject matter; used properly, they grab the readers and generate interest in reading by creating curiosity. In this manner, something like, "AN ALTERNATE HEARING AID POWER SOURCE," is descriptive, but dull and unexciting. More likely to motivate readers to look within is, "COAL-FIRED HEARING AIDS."

Who could resist leafing through a document with that title? If only to find out what kind of lunatic would think of such a bizarre device, people will want to read what follows.

In letters, a "title" can be provided in the form of a subject callout above the text. Like report or proposal titles, callouts should identify the subject matter, but in a way that generates reader interest. Were your boss the stingiest employer in town, for example, he would probably not feel compelled to put great priority on an interoffice memo preceded by,

SUBJECT: Salary Increases

The *last* thing he wants is to pay raises, so this might be the last thing he reads. But why not go right for the jugular and grab his attention at the beginning by forcing him to draw an inference more to his liking? All you need do is to change your subject heading to,

SUBJECT: Eliminating Salary Increases

That will flag him down. He won't be able to resist finding out how he can avoid giving out pay raises. If you then proceed in your text to show how eliminating salary increases would be counter-productive and lead to wholesale resignations, that's your business.

When multiple topics must be covered in one letter, subject callouts head off confusion by up front identification of what is about to be discussed:

SUBJECT: Answers to the Ten Questions Listed in Your April 4 Memo

With two exceptions, every document should have a subject or title. Callouts are optional if a letter or note is short enough so that the entire text can be seen as quickly as the title. Also, if subject identification is likely to turn readers away, or if attention-getting callouts might be considered too gimmicky for certain readers, go directly to a strong opening without a callout.

Start Strong

A strong beginning seizes reader attention if you don't yet have it, or keeps it if you do. Try this one on for size:

Mr. George Washington
123 Fourth Street
Valley Forge, FL   56789

Dear Mr. Washington:

How would you like the best vacation deal of your life?

This sentence comes right out with an appeal to Washington's instinctive need to enjoy himself, but it's a bad opening. It is bad because it invites him to say, "NO!" at the beginning. Perhaps Washington believes that all "best deal of your life" offers are come-ons with no substance. Or, he may have just returned from a vacation.

But suppose he would have wanted to use the writer's services for business purposes? Suppose the writer didn't mention until the fifth paragraph that the deal being offered was a trip to Florida for $36? Too bad; Washington threw away the letter as soon as he said, "NO!"

"Can we solve your investment problems?" is another beauty. Friend Washington reads that and says to himself: "What problems? I have no problems!" He may *not* say that and he may not lack interest in the vacation deal either, but why risk it? If you are offering something great, say so up front with an opening sentence such as: "Florida for $36. Here's how."

Even if curiosity is your only ally, the letter will be read.

Don't ever give readers an opportunity to say, "NO!" at the outset. By doing so, you also give them a chance to disassociate themselves with everything else that follows and to deposit your document in the cylindrical file beside their desks.

Another opening to avoid is one that does not get immediately to the point. Several potential problems might crop up if you wrote a first paragraph such as:

> Dear Mr. Washington:
>
> Please accept my thanks for taking the time and trouble to meet with me yesterday. Not always will a person in your position be willing to interrupt his busy schedule to discuss matters un-related to his day-to-day activities and you can be assured that your cooperation was very much appreciated.

When Washington gets this far, he may assume that the primary purpose of your letter was to express your appreciation. In the event that his telephone then rings, or should someone then walk into his office, the interruption may divert his attention. After that, there may be a succession of diversions. He hasn't necessarily forgotten you, but from the way you started, he was given no reason for perceiving your letter as containing a matter of high priority urgency in the next-to-last paragraph.

Some people read every word and every punctuation mark of every document that comes in, but those people are in the minority. Most of us skim, look for the high spots, study what we think is important and read nothing else. Still others start with the first word and read in sequence to the last. You may know which approach a specific reader usually takes, but you never know the extent to which events may cause a reader to be interrupted and *not* see your key points at first glance.

Anticipate the worst. Assume that readers will be interrupted, distracted and interrupted again. Far from being contrived, such a situation is commonplace for busy men like Washington. If you don't get their attention right away, you may never get it.

What if the prime purpose of your letter was to get his immediate approval on an important matter? What if you didn't mention that matter until the sixth paragraph? What if he doesn't get past the first paragraph for a week? You could (and probably should) call as a backup, but if you want to write first and if you feel strongly about thanking him up front, do it quickly.

> Dear Mr. Washington:
>
> Thanks for meeting me yesterday. Our discussion was interesting, but I believe that your immediate attention is still required on the following items: . . .

To find out which items you mean, he'll have no choice but to continue reading.

Even better, skip the thanks until later and start directly with a direct assault:

> Dear Mr. Washington:
>
> Subsequent to our meeting yesterday, my accounting department identified four areas that require your immediate attention: . . .

Which areas? Why do they require immediate attention? Sorry, Mr. Washington, you're going to have to read the rest of the letter to find out.

Except for very short notes, a good first paragraph should create interest without giving away the whole message. Ask yourself what will whet the reader's appetite and which incentives the reader would like to find out about. Someone seeking a job might start out with:

Dear Mr. Washington:

Currently the marketing manager for one of your competitors, I was responsible for the award-winning advertising program you have undoubtedly seen recently in all the major trade journals serving our industry. As you may already know, this program has resulted in a significant sales growth during the past three months.

Will Washington hire this person? Who knows? He'd want to have more information before making a job offer. But he will read the rest of the letter; he won't be able to resist finding out something about the competition and why the writer is looking to change jobs.

Don't need a job? Perhaps you can use this opening:

Dear Mr. Washington:

You are absolutely correct.

If he has any ego at all, there's no way Washington will be able to resist finding out *why* you think he's right.

Another technique is to start out with something like:

Dear Mr. Washington:

In accordance with section 17, paragraph 3 of our agreement, several procedural changes have to be made this week.

What on earth is in section 17, paragraph 3? What changes have to be made? He'll have to read further to find out, won't he?

Subdividing

Readabilitycouldnotexistwithoutsubdividingbooksinto chapterschaptersintosectionssectionsintoparagraphsparagraphs intosentencesandsentencesintowordseliminatesubdivisionsand readerswouldnotknowwhenonewordbeginsandanotherendsthey alsowouldnotknowwhenoneideaendsandthenextonestartsifa readercannotdistinguishideasfromoneanothertransferringthose ideasisimpossible

Need a translation? Subdivide!

> Readability could not exist without subdividing books into chapters, chapters into sections, sections into paragraphs, paragraphs into sentences, and sentences into words. Eliminate subdivisions and readers would not know when one word begins and another ends. They also would not know when one idea ends and the next one starts. If a reader cannot distinguish ideas from one another, transferring those ideas is impossible.

That's a big improvement, but notice how much easier the message is read if it is split into three paragraphs:

> Readability could not exist without subdividing books into chapters, chapters into sections, sections into paragraphs, paragraphs into sentences, and sentences into words.
>
> Eliminate subdivisions and readers would not know when one word begins and another ends. They also would not know when one idea ends and the next one starts.
>
> If a reader cannot distinguish ideas from one another, transferring those ideas is impossible.

Subdividing is like cutting food into small portions that can be readily consumed. Do people consume sides of beef in one swallow? Certainly not—beef is cut into servings, which are in turn cut by each person during the dining process. Without all the cutting, beef could not be efficiently consumed, eating would not be enjoyable, and a lot of us would give up, thinking the rewards to be not worth the effort. So why make readers "choke" on your ideas? Subdivide; convey your message in small chunks that a reader's mind will find digestible.

Start by expressing yourself with the shortest, easiest understood words, and by writing sentences that can be read and understood at a glance. If you find yourself writing a sentence longer than three lines, break the sentence up; many sentences that long are too difficult to comprehend without rereading.

The same goes for paragraphs. When readers skim, they tend to "see" the first two or three lines and the last two or three lines of a paragraph. As a result, long paragraphs tend to submerge information more than four lines in. For highlighting information rather than burying it, maximum paragraph length is ideally no more than six lines. Longer paragraphs must be written with care to make sure that critical information is not hidden from the skimmer's limited visibility.

"One subject at a time" applies to subdivisions as much as it does to a complete document. Each subdivision must deal only with those ideas that have a strong commonality of topic, and each should be restricted to one or more aspects of the topic covered in the next larger subdivision. A paragraph, for example, must have a clear subject matter focus, and any sentence in that paragraph must deal only with some aspect of that subject.

The paragraph you just finished, for example, talked about grouping subdivisions by topic. The paragraph before that, on the other hand, spoke of paragraph maximum length guidelines, while the paragraph before that spoke of sentence length limitations. Now, you are in the midst of a paragraph whose purpose is to point out examples of subdividing by topic.

So even if paragraph length is not excessive, when the topic changes, start a new paragraph; clustering by topic helps readers to identify and follow your meaning in coherent, logical thoughts.

One Thing Leads to Another

People are more likely to agree with your conclusions if they can follow and agree with your train of thought. Your thinking should be immediately obvious as a logical sequence of events, ideas, or relationships. Otherwise, a reader may be diverted from thinking about your incentives to figuring out your logic.

Readability suffers whenever a writer—

1. states conclusions long before they are justified or explained;
2. asks for action before answering the "What's in it for me?" question;
3. jumps in and out of chronological order;
4. fails to relate cause directly to effect;

5. fails to demonstrate relevance at any point where readers may ask, "Why is this being discussed here?"

If one thing leads to another, show *how* it leads, and do it right there, not three paragraphs down or four pages later. The following memo is a case in point!

We will have to open our new office in Perth Amboy rather than in Bayonne. I have therefore asked several Perth Amboy realtors to call you next week so that you can arrange to visit and select a suitable location.

Only twenty-five miles south of Bayonne, Perth Amboy has a number of new office buildings ready for immediate occupancy at attractive rates, excellent access to all major highways, and close proximity to the airport. This change should therefore have no detrimental effect on our plans.

I am sorry to impose additional office selection duties on you at this time, but the situation in Bayonne could not have been anticipated. We were told only three days ago that the facilities there will not be ready until six months after we plan to open. We therefore have no choice but to go elsewhere if we are to maintain our schedule.

The memo is complete and contains all the information necessary to understand what the writer is after, but only by a roundabout route:

1. The opening paragraph states a conclusion about not opening in Bayonne, but the reasoning behind that conclusion is not given until the third paragraph.

2. The first paragraph also states that the office will be opened in Perth Amoy, but the acceptability of that city is not justified until the second paragraph.

3. Before the facts on either city are given, the reader is asked to take action.

To follow this writer's train of thought, we therefore have to travel from the first paragraph to the third, then back to first, to the second, back again to the first, and then to the third once more.

Imagine how confusing this kind of writing would be in a long proposal!

Here's how the office location memo should look:

> We were told three days ago that the new facilities in Bayonne will not be ready until six months after we plan to open.
>
> I have discovered, however, that we can open on time in Perth Amboy, which is only twenty-five miles south of Bayonne and has a number of new office buildings ready for immediate occupancy at attractive rates. Perth Amboy also has excellent access to all major highways, and close proximity to the airport, so this change should have no detrimental effect on our plans.
>
> I have asked several Perth Amboy realtors to call you next week. Please arrange to meet with them so as to select a suitable location. Sorry to impose this extra work on you, but the situation in Bayonne could not have been anticipated and we now have no choice but to open elsewhere if we are to maintain our schedule.

Now, there is no need to hopscotch through the paragraphs to follow the writer's logic:

1. The first paragraph stands on its own in informing us what has happened in Bayonne.

2. The second paragraph goes right into telling us about another city, and then explains why that city is an acceptable alternative.

3. The third paragraph indicates what is expected of the reader and clearly answers the "What's in it for me?" question.

Self-contained with a full explanation, each paragraph covers a different aspect of the overall story, which is presented in a sequence that allows an easy flow of ideas.

But rather than being written in a "one thing leads to another" manner, the Bayonne-Perth Amboy story might be looked upon as more of a "one thing stems from another" situation. Yet other messages could be "one thing adds to another," "one thing precedes or follows another," or "one thing is conditional on another." Either way, conclusions must be given in close proximity to explanations, causes shown right next to effects, and facts presented in what readers will perceive as a logical, easy-to-follow sequence.

Continuity

Within a paragraph, or at the juncture between paragraphs, one thing will lead to another only if writing has continuity—a smooth flow of information from one idea to the next. A logical progression of ideas always helps, but even with that, several techniques—often in combination with each other—can be used to help tie sentences and paragraphs to one another:

Repetition of Words or Word Patterns. Successive sentences can be thought-connected by use of the same word in each: "We recently purchased a new computer for our Denver office. That computer is the one we used to handle our advertising letters," or the same word pattern: "Last year, we were struggling to break even. This year, we have more business than we can handle."

Use of Antecedents to Refer Back to the Previous Sentence. Two sentences like: "Six months ago, I hired Jane to run our New York office. She is doing a great job," have continuity because *she*—in the second sentence—refers directly to *Jane* in the first sentence.

Transitioning to Show How Ideas Are Connected. Expressions such as *however, on the other hand, for example, for instance, furthermore, in other words, as a result, in this case,* and *in conclusion* smooth the path between ideas. The following paragraph uses no transitional expressions:

> You can use several types of transitions. Many people do not take advantage of the continuity techniques at their disposal. Their writing has a tedious cadence. This paragraph is dull and borrrrring.

But this version does.

You can use several types of transitions. Many people, however, do not take advantage of the continuity techniques at their disposal. As a result, their writing has a tedious cadence. Note how smooth this paragraph is compared to the previous one.

Now we can see that the second sentence is presented in contrast to the first, and that the third sentence summarizes what came before it. By providing a "thought bridge" between ideas, the transitions therefore provide a smooth flow between ideas and soften the staccato manner in which those ideas would otherwise have to be digested.

Placing Elaborative Sentences Immediately After Those that Need Justifying. An elaborative sentence justifies the validity of its predecessor. Examples are:

Jim doesn't look good. *He is worried about his father's upcoming kidney operation.*

I am concerned about our performance this year. *Profits are far below expectations.*

In each case, the second sentence justifies the first sentence's validity. Specifically, the elaborative sentences indicate *why* Jim doesn't look good and *why* the writer is concerned about performance. Well-written elaborations answer questions so directly that readers have no cause to "stop and think" about anything.

Resequencing Sentences for Better Idea Flow. Many sentences can be written in alternate sequences without changing words or meaning. A typical example is, "You can retire tomorrow if you win the lottery today," which can also be written as, "If you win the lottery today, you can retire tomorrow."

Both versions are equally understandable. Which one to use, however, depends on circumstances. If the sentence were to be followed by another talking about the virtues of moving to California, the clumsy approach would be to say: "You can retire tomorrow if you win the lottery today. Then, you could move to California and live in a beach house."

Here, the sequence is out of whack. Moving to California comes after retiring, which must come after (not before) winning the lottery. The proper order is therefore: "If you win the lottery today, you can retire tomorrow. Then, you could move to California and live in a beach house."

Grabbers. Every so often, you'll do yourself a favor by ending or beginning a paragraph with a "grabber"—a sentence that acts as bait to motivate people to read further. Can you think of a typical grabber technique?

You just saw one. If it's provocative, a question at the end of one paragraph will motivate readers to go on to the next paragraph to get the answer. As long as that answer is the first sentence of that next paragraph, the scheme will work without creating negatives.

Other "grabbers" are typified by sentences such as:

- The following sentences illustrate "grabbers."
- He had to change his plans.
- I have come to an important conclusion.
- It had only one problem.

What sentences? What was the change? What conclusion? What problem? The only way to find out is to read further.

Don't Look Back

Refer back to previous paragraphs or pages only if they are more than a page away in a document more than two or three pages long. Starting a sentence with, "As discussed earlier, . . ." means nothing because the reader is not told how much earlier, and saying, "As discussed in the last paragraph, . . ." says that you think the reader is an idiot for not being able to remember what was discussed only a few lines earlier.

Should a prior statement be necessary or helpful, it can be referenced, but the reference should be specific at least as far as page number, and a reason should be given for referencing: "As shown on page 15, our facilities are capable of accommodating additional equipment and additional work."

Going from one thing to another is fine. Going back again, however, can be counterproductive. A given argument, viewpoint, incentive, or illustration should be presented as effectively as possible: once. This does not mean that certain points cannot be summarized in a concluding statement or paragraph, but rather that a weak argument gets no stronger by being repeated unchanged. Nor in the context of a single document does an incentive become more attractive by being stated again and again.

A different slant on that argument, on the other hand, is new information, which is admissible in any logical sequence. Different aspects of a position may therefore show up in different sections of a text depending upon how each aspect relates to the topics being discussed.

In your writing, state each position as well as you can, and make each point as effectively as you can. After that, move on to another position and another point. Never repeat an argument without adding a new slant, never repeat an incentive without providing new evidence as to its value, and never give the impression that you have little to offer except a lot of duplication.

Having stated your case in the most effective manner, you need be concerned only that your incentives will be noticed and your logic seen. The following sections will help you to highlight and emphasize key points so they can't be missed.

Getting Attention with Headlines

The four boldfaced words above this sentence are a headline. Like other headlines, it announces the content of the material that follows. By being spaced apart from the text and printed in a different size and style of type, it also attracts attention to that material.

A headline is called a primary headline if it is used on a line by itself, double-spaced away from the text. All chapters and sections in this book are flagged by primary headlines.

With a secondary headline, however, the text starts immediately after (often on the same line as) the headline. Secondary headlines can merely announce that text, as is the case with the subject callouts discussed on page 99, or they can precede the text and be a part of it, a was done on pages 25–27 in describing writing objectives.

Surrounded by blank space, primary headlines stand out more, but secondary headlines take up less room. Primary headlines are used for titles and main subdivisions like chapters or sections, whereas secondary headlines usually are used for paragraphs or paragraph groups within sections. In a short document such as a letter, secondary headlines are generally all that is necessary.

Listed in a table of contents, chapter headlines allow readers to rapidly find out which subjects are covered on which pages. When main subdivisions are easy to find, they are more likely to be found, and certainly more likely to be read.

Word Highlighting

Headlines, as well as words within sentences, can be highlighted by underlining, by boldfacing, by using different typestyles such as *italics*, by printing all CAPITAL LETTERS, by switching to a colored typewriter ribbon, or by adding color during printing. In addition, sentences can be "punctuated" with quotation marks just to make certain words or phrases stand out.

Highlighting headlines can also be accomplished by using large-size type, but most documents have no room for oversize lettering in single-spaced text. Undersize lettering? It would draw attention and might be fine in a flashy advertisement, but for business correspondence, it would be inappropriate.

Number Highlighting

Numbers can be written out as words or presented as figures, so this book can be described as having ten chapters or 10 chapters, depending on who is doing the describing.

Most writing books say that for contemporary usage, spell out numbers less than 100, numbers at the beginning of a sentence, and "round" numbers that are intended as approximations. Numerical figures, on the other hand, are recommended for numbers greater than 100; for dates; for addresses; for chapter or figure numbers; and for fractions, decimals, and percentages. *A Manual of Style* (see Bibliography), for example, has more than eight pages on choosing between figures or words when writing numbers.

In getting and keeping a reader's attention, however, one must think rather than follow "rules" with blind obedience. No one will get confused by numbers shown as figures, but a sentence such as, "I bought twelve sixteen-pound turkeys," would cause anyone to come to a halt to figure out what the numbers mean. The sentence should be replaced by, "I bought twelve 16-pound turkeys," or, "I bought 12 sixteen-pound turkeys."

That which stands out the most is that which is most unlike everything else. When everything else in a sentence is made up of words, the best way to make a number stand out is to write it as a figure. Keep in mind, however, that figures often look less imposing than their word counterparts. Accordingly, *seventy-seven cents*, which uses up seventeen letters and two spaces, may to some readers take on more emphasis than *77¢*. Similarly, *18 miles* may to some eyes seem like less of a distance than *eighteen miles*, while *eight thousand seven hundred fifty five dollars* may look like a fortune compared to the paltry sum of *$8,755*.

Between figures, words, underlining, and the other word-highlighting schemes just described, you have a wide choice of ways to emphasize or de-emphasize numbers. In doubt as to which choice to take? Try each in a draft and then use those gizmos on either side of your nose to see which option best suits your purpose.

Lists

Names, places, objects, events, dollar amounts, and other items frequently are listed in a series, but the result in continuous text is that each entry is not well highlighted, as in:

> We have nine paid holidays annually: January 1, Lincoln's Birthday, Washington's Birthday, Memorial Day, July 4, Labor Day,

> Thanksgiving, the day after Thanksgiving, and Christmas. Also, three additional paid holidays can be chosen and taken by each employee with more than one-year's service.

The paragraph is clearly written, but it has to be read carefully to note each date. If it is read too quickly, the paragraph also might hide the fact that after a year, employees get three more days off. See how much easier each holiday is to spot when the information is presented in a two-column vertical list:

> We have nine paid holidays annually:
>
> –January 1   –Labor Day
> –Lincoln's Birthday   –Thanksgiving
> –Washington's Birthday   –Day after Thanksgiving
> –Memorial Day   –Christmas
> –July 4
>
> Also, three additional paid holidays can be chosen and taken by each employee with more than one-year's service.

Now, each item "pops" out of the page at you, and even the three extra days are more prominently featured. Each listed holiday is introduced with a dash to indicate commonality with the other listed items. This is therefore known as a dash list. Note that list is double-columned, but this is to save space. Note also that the listed items are single-spaced, yet each stands out. If space allows, even more readability can be achieved by double-spacing dash lists.

When sequence or rank order is important, another type of vertical list is the enumerated list, such as the following one that tabulates the results of a summer bowling league:

> After completing our 14-week season, the standings and average scores for each team are:
> 1. State National Bank (682)
> 2. Fryer's (655)
> 3. CJ's Restaurant (644)
> 4. Red's Gas (612)
> 5. Barton's Real Estate (598)
> 6. Collegiates (594)
> 7. Avery Trucking (591)

If listed items have no chronological order and no numerical order, they can be identified by letters or numbers for future reference. In a long document, readability might therefore be aided if you can reference back to something like "item F on the list shown on page 54."

The trouble with vertical lists is that they can take up lots of vertical space. If multiple columns or single-spacing do not reduce list size to the amount of space you have, try presenting the list in a continuous series, but leave space between each entry and number or letter the listed items:

> We have nine paid holidays annually: *1.* New Year's Day, *2.* Lincoln's Birthday, *3.* Washington's Birthday, *4.* Memorial Day, *5.* July 4, *6.* Labor Day, *7.* Thanksgiving, *8.* Day after Thanksgiving, *9.* Christmas.
>
> Also, three additional paid holidays can be chosen and taken by each employee with more than one-year's service.

This version takes up more lines than the original version, but has far greater readability. The vertical-dash list has even greater readability, but it takes up even more space. Which is best for you? Try each and then choose.

A list is but another form of subdivision; its function is to make certain words stand out. Do not, however, think that listing is restricted to a large number of items. Any of these techniques can be used with a list consisting of as few as two entries.

Tables

A table consists of one or more vertical lists positioned adjacent to one another in such a way that the lists relate on a line-by-line basis. Some tables compare the lists, as does this one evaluating salesman performance.

Salesman	Johnson	Posner
Sales territory	New York	Chicago
Years on job	14	4
Sales last year	$671,000	$514,000
Number of orders last year	2,118	1,351

While in some tables the lists elaborate on each other, as shown in the following table:

June Expenses	Amount	Explanation
Roof repair	$11,350	Budgeted maintenance
Word processors	6,687	Three systems for new Chicago office
Window replacements	890	Wind damage
Carpentry	3,309	Upper tier of warehouse office
Travel	449	Inspection of Dallas field office
	$22,685	

A table may not be able to tell the whole story about anything, but it can say in a graphic manner what would otherwise require several paragraphs or several pages.

Should you choose to tailor and to sidestep negatives while tabulating data, you can list only those comparisons or elaborations that help your argument while submerging other information within accompanying paragraphs. In the case of the Johnson versus Posner sales performance comparison, Johnson clearly looks like the more productive salesman, but suppose his performance has been slipping over the years while Posner's has been steadily improving. Depending on how much damage you do or do not want inflicted on Johnson, you can include trend data in the table, show it in a graph or say nothing about trends.

As with any other readability technique, the question with tables is, "What do you want to 'jump out' at the reader and what would you rather keep to yourself or hide someplace where it will have minimum impact?"

Emphasize with Positioning

If important information is surrounded by words on all sides, it may be missed by readers who skim. Accordingly, short paragraphs, highlighting, and dash-lists are used to make key points stand out no matter where they are located.

Another approach is to position those points at the top or bottom of a paragraph. Rather than being buried within a mass of other words, the information to be emphasized is thereby located adjacent to a blank line and easier to spot. To illustrate the advantages of positioning, here are the closing paragraphs in a cover letter of the type that might accompany a computer proposal:

> In accordance with your request of July 6, we are therefore pleased to submit the enclosed proposal for providing, installing and programming a TURBODATA computer for your offices.
>
> Powered by the exhaust from the heating system in your building, your TURBODATA computer will reduce data processing energy consumption by 30 percent. Our equipment is available this month at 40 percent off list price, so you will start saving money even before the unit is turned on. Also, we will refund half our programming fee if the system is used in accordance with our instructions and fails to increase your data handling productivity.
>
> We look forward to your early favorable reply. Should you have any questions, contact me at any time.

The problem with these paragraphs is that the wrong information is position highlighted. The energy savings, the discount, and the refund are deep within the text, while, "and programming a TURBODATA computer for your offices," "powered by the exhaust from the heating system in your building," and "instructions and fails to increase your data-handling productivity," are prominently featured along with the short last paragraph. Highlighting failures while hiding a refund offer makes no sense; the material should be rewritten as follows:

> In accordance with your request of July 6, we are therefore pleased to submit the enclosed proposal for providing, installing and programming a TURBODATA computer. Our entire line is available this month at 40 percent off list price.
>
> Your data processing energy consumption will be reduced by 30 percent because the TURBODATA computer will be powered by the exhaust from the heating system in your building. Also, if the system is used in accordance with our instructions and fails to increase your data handling productivity, we will refund half our programming fee.
>
> We look forward to your early favorable reply. Should you have any questions, contact me at any time.

Now located on a line by itself next to an empty line, each of the incentives is less likely to be missed.

Stand-Alones

Slogans, equations, and quotations can be highlighted within paragraphs by double-spacing them away from the surrounding text. The same can be done to emphasize examples of items such as titles, names, or—as done throughout this book—different kinds of sentences. Just be sure to keep in mind that,

Why is this information emphasized?

is a question that you should anticipate and answer with an immediate elaborative sentence before questions can be asked and negatives generated.

Graphics

Charts, figures, drawings, and photographs are great for illustrating information, but they should never be clustered together at the end of a long document. Ideally, graphics should be described and located on the same page, but if that isn't feasible, they should be located no more than a page away from their descriptions. All figures should also be captioned and numbered for easy reference.

There's no problem with clustering graphics if your are—

1. adding two charts or figures to a one-page letter;

2. sending a group of photographs with a short letter;

3. using a number of graphics that do not need individual descriptions.

But most figures in most reports and proposals do need individual descriptions. If those descriptions are positioned in the text so that readers constantly have to flip back and forth across a span of pages, you are building in a diversion that is likely to result in a resounding negative.

Variations

On page 108, examples were given to illustrate how repetition can be used to good advantage in providing continuity. But too much of anything is likely to lead to trouble. Repetition must be used sparingly and systematically, because if everything looks like everything else, nothing stands out. When that happens, all or part of a document is characterized by sameness, a quality that can put readers to sleep if it first doesn't motivate them to do or read something else. The following guidelines will help to insure that you write in a lively style:

- Avoid needless duplication of word usage. You'd be better off to paraphrase, substitute different words, use alternate wording, rephrase, restate, reword, use synonyms or find another way to make your point.

If these techniques fail, try coming up with a replacement of equivalent meaning.

- Should you find no acceptable substitute for word combinations that must be stated more than once, try changing the sequence in which those words are used.

~~Repetition~~ Duplication of word usage can be a problem because sentences and paragraphs beginning with a given expression can be misaken for other ~~sentences and paragraphs~~ paragraphs and sentences ~~beginning~~ starting with the same terminology.

- Do not write a string of the same length sentences or a string of the same length paragrpahs.

- Give each paragraph its own identity by writing it in a form different from that of its neighbors. Both of these paragraphs have essentially the same structure:

In accordance with Figure 1, sales were significantly up in the south and southwest. In the northeast and midwest, however, new orders were essentially unchanged from the previous year. As a result, our domestic performance was only slightly better than was planned.

As shown in Figure 2, We did well in England, South America, and Japan last year. Bookings in Europe and the Middle East, on the other hand, declined. Accordingly, total international sales did not increase as fast as domestic sales.

1. A first sentence introduced by a prepositional phrase and ending with a clause that talks about the areas in which sales were up.

2. A second sentence that tells where sales were down or unchanged. In the first paragraph, *however* is used to present the second sentence as contrasting with the first. The second paragraph takes the same route by using *on the other hand*, which has the same meaning as *however*.

3. A third and final sentence that draws a conclusion from the preceding sentences. Both third sentences begin with a transitional expression.

There is nothing wrong with either of the two paragraphs, but together they have a "sing-song" effect that may be more memorable for having a repeated cadence than it is for the content of each paragraph. To make the information stand out more than the rhythm pattern, one paragraph (or both) should be rewritten.

In accordance with Figure 1, sales were significantly up in the south and southwest, but unchanged from the previous year in the northeast and midwest. Overall, however, domestic performance was slightly better than was planned.

International sales, Figure 2, did not increase as fast as domestic sales last year; bookings declined in Europe and the Middle East but we did well in England, South America, and Japan.

- Occasionally surprise readers by using one-word paragraphs or one-sentence paragraphs to emphasize key points.

People generally think of paragraphs as containing a series of sentences that discuss different aspects of a common theme, but sameness in paragraph length can lead readers to mistakenly think that "look-alikes" in size are equal in importance. Long paragraphs may bury information, but can extremely short paragraphs help?

Absolutely!

As long as a sentence transfers an idea, it need not have more than one word.

Don't Get Carried Away

Tell some people to emphasize key points and they highlight everything to the point where nothing stands out. Readers get no sense of priority if you use too many vertical lists, too many tiny paragraphs, too many headlines, or too much underlining.

So control yourself and highlight only the critical items. You are probably getting carried away if you underline more than five or six words per page or if you use one-word paragraphs more frequently than once every five or ten pages.

Multiple headlines are OK in sales promotion letters, but be leery of using more than two headlines in a typical one-page business letter. Ask yourself whether such a letter is focused enough, or whether it should be split into separate letters for each topic discussed.

Also, every topic shift does not need its own headline. Use headlines only for the most important sections. A letter with several paragraphs, for instance, may have one paragraph that you want read above all else. Fine; introduce it with a headline.

Keep in mind, however, that one headline won't work (or could cause confusion) if it is followed by a different topic that has no headline. In the last section of a document, however, single headlines are a fine way to draw attention to crucial matters.

Only one headline? Why not? Where is it written that headlines in the text must have the same count as topic groupings?

No place. There are also no commandments against emphasizing by using a paragraph constructed of three questions, but having just read such a paragraph, you'd get bored by seeing one like it on every page.

Avoiding repetition is another task at which you should not get carried away. An "epistolarian," for example, is nothing more than a letter writer, but who ever hear of an "epistolarian"? There are many words (*paragraph* is a good example) for which there are no good substitutes. Fine—so repeat such words. If you have to repeat, you have to repeat and doing so is a lot better than dredging up words no one will understand.

Should you find yourself using a particular readability technique too often, take another look at the chapter you've just finished.

There are so many ways to get and keep reader attention that you can always take a different tact.

8

LETTERS AND MEMOS

For convincing or motivating, the most effective letter/memo format is based on a technique first developed to get people to notice and read advertisements. As adapted to one-on-one correspondence, that format consists of four elements usually presented in an *ACBC* sequence:

A. Get the Reader's Attention. Compel the reader to read what follows. A host of attention-getting techniques were discussed in chapter 7. You must maintain reader attention throughout, but if you don't capture it at the beginning, you may wind up talking to yourself.

C. Make a Claim. State or imply the idea or concept you wish to transfer. A claim can be as bold as a boast or as subtle as an implication that a particular idea has validity.

B. Back it Up. Justify or explain the claim; give the reader reasons and incentives as may be necessary for him to accept the claim. Go to the bottom line.

C. Call for action. Indicate what you want the reader to do, what you will do, or both.

The length of any one of these elements can vary depending upon the situation. Some letters might best get attention with a one-word subject callout headline, others with the first sentence of an opening paragraph, and still others with a short sentence functioning as a paragraph by itself. The same goes for claims and backup information; some instances may require only a few words while others may need several paragraphs.

Making a claim can by itself attract reader attention. A memo* that starts with a claim such as, "My November 9 memo to you is in error," would, if addressed to you, get your attention because you would want to look further to see what the mistake was. That claim could then be explained with, "Rather than thirty dollars, your December commission check will be for three hundred dollars," and ended with a call for action indicating what you should do next: "Please let me know if you have not received our check in that amount within ten days."

As a result, the entire *ACBC* format can be laid out within the confines of a three-sentence paragraph:

> My November 9 memo to you was in error. Rather than thirty dollars, your December commission check will be for three hundred dollars. Please let me know if you have not received our check in that amount within ten days.

The following letter also uses the *ACBC* format, but in more traditional multiparagraph form. Format element names are provided in italics to help you identify how they are used.

A. *Get the Reader's Attention*
    You must be kidding!

C. *Make a Claim*
    The value of our Ninth-Street property is considerably higher than the hundred thousand dollars you offered in your letter of August 5.

---

*A memo is a letter sent to someone with whom the writer has a close enough relationship to justify informal (first-name basis) addressing, and signing. Examples are interoffice correspondence and personal notes.

B. *Back it Up* (backup reasons highlighted by being listed)
Specifically,

—the land alone is assessed at current tax levels at
$90,000;

—the tax assessment on the building is assessed on the
basis of a $85,000-valuation;

—these figures do not reflect recent refinishing and
plumbing renovations, which combined would increase
the value of the building by at least 40 percent;

—we last month rejected as insufficient two offers that were
nearly double yours.

C. *Call for Action*
Should you be willing and able to submit a more suitable
offer, we would be willing to give it serious consideration.

"You must be kidding!" attracts attention because it is out-
rageous. "The value of our Ninth-Street property is considerably
higher than the hundred thousand dollars you offered in your letter
of August 5," will also attract attention, however, because the
reader will naturally want to know why his offer was considered
low. Which opening is best depends on the situation and on the
relationship between writer and reader. "You must be kidding"
could be offensive to a conservative stranger.

You always have a choice of whether to use a standalone attention-
getter or to attract reader interest by virtue of how you state your
opening claim. Look for such choices and try them out in draft form
before deciding what to do.

Justify Only What Needs Justifying

"Back it up" does not mean explaining or justifying every statement or implication made in a letter; it means explaining to the
reader why he should believe you and obey you. This means giving

incentives, which is what chapters 2 and 3 were all about. In accordance with chapter 5, it also means avoiding statements or implications that could result in unanswered questions that in turn could lead to negatives.

It does not, however, mean that every statement or implication has to be backed up, explained or justified. Stating that, "Our next meeting is scheduled for April 24 at 2:00 P.M. in my office," is to state a fact. Does that fact have to be justified? Only if a reader is likely to doubt its validity. If the time or place might be considered unusual or surprising, justify; likewise if the purpose of the letter is to clarify the time or place. But if your primary objective is to get people to be at the meeting, and if there is little or no chance that where or when will be questioned, what you must justify is the reader being in attendance.

Statements need be justified only when convincing or motivating is liable to be necessary. In the formats just described, the claim of a letter is the idea that you want a reader to accept. Back up that claim in detail, but if you must state or imply facts, do not feel obligated to explain them all; explain only those that hinge on idea acceptance *and* that need elaboration to avoid creating negatives.

For example, a conclusion or opinion like, "We can finish by Friday if the pictures are developed tonight," needs no back up unless a reader would have reason to think it to be unbelievable.

When a letter or memo is written only to inform, the main claim may need no backup section.

> You were correct.
>
> Removing the ground connection eliminated the interference we had been experiencing from FM radio signals.
>
> Thanks for the help. We will now be moving on to the remote control phase of our experiments. I'll keep you posted on progress.

This claim is the result of following the reader's previous recommendations, and no backup is required for an understanding of what is meant.

If in this example another purpose were to request additional help, the claim-backup process would have to be started anew, as in:

You were correct.

Removing the ground connection eliminated the interference we had been experiencing from FM radio signals.

We now have another problem in that power consumption is excessive in the solenoid circuitry. Rather than operating at the 3-watt level anticipated by our engineers, the system has been drawing 18 watts at full power. Unfortunately, this is almost 3 times the capacity we can build in for portable operation by batteries.

Next week we are going to attempt use of a fuel cell to increase internal power generation. The cell will be here on Tuesday and our test is scheduled for Wednesday.

Please arrange to be here to witness this important test. Your presence will insure us of the ability to perform on-the-spot evaluations and to establish and modify the setup as required to complete our work before the week is out.

Let me know of your flight plans and I will pick you up at the airport.

Here, the six paragraphs constitute yet another variation on the *ACBC* format. The first two paragraphs—an attention-getter followed by a claim needing no backup—are the same as those used in the previous example. The call for action, however, does not take place until the fourth paragraph, after another claim is made in the third paragraph.

The fifth paragraph then includes a second call for action and yet another claim, while the last paragraph is a third call for action. Backup is provided only when not doing so might generate negatives, but each claim is followed by a call for action.

Once the reader's attention is sought with a good opener, the letter in essence represents a series of "Here's where things stand" claims, followed by "Here's why (or how) things are as they are" backups when necessary, and then by "Here's what should be done about it" calls for action.

The *ACBC* format, like any other writing technique, is a tool for your use, not a straitjacket in which you must confine your writing. If what you do gets and keeps the reader's attention, goes to the bottom line, and ends with the reader thinking about what you want, you've got a good format regardless of the liberties you may choose to take with the basic *ACBC* approach.

Storytelling

Aside from wanting to motivate, inform or express feelings, you may want to tell a story in writing—not in the sense of fairy tales or fiction, but in the sense of relating a sequence of events that lead the reader to a specific conclusion that you would like reached.

This kind of storytelling is best accomplished as the *B* part of an *ACBC* letter by using a sequence of events to back up a claim which in reality is the conclusion you want reached. An example is a trip report of the type a salesman might submit to his boss after calling on an important customer:

> As a result of a productive call I made on Shipner Motors yesterday, they are about to place a large order with us.
>
> The call was originally scheduled because Harry Stewart, Shipner's new owner, had complained about what he claimed was excessive repairs his customers were experiencing on our clutch assemblies. Harry is an important customer, so I rushed over there to see what the problem was.
>
> After spending two hours in his service department, there was no question in my mind that his people were installing our clutches properly. So I then went through his parts book and found out what was happening.
>
> Apparently, his parts manager had lost our new catalog and was using the one we printed last year. As a result, they were not ordering the correct parts from us. We had changed our design last year and the parts they have been ordering were simply the wrong parts for many of the new cars Shipner has been servicing.
>
> Harry was thrilled when I told him that the "problem" was a simple mixup that was easily solved. He was also pleased with our quick assistance. As a result, he gave me a letter of intent (copy attached) to use exclusively for all of his transmission and engine parts. Since he has eight dealerships in the tri-state area, his business will therefore easily triple what it was last year.

> Firm purchase orders and parts inventory requirements will be in from Harry within the next seven to ten days.

This entire memo is nothing more than an attention-getting claim followed by a backup that ends with a call for action that indicates what will happen next.

Storytelling can also be used to lead readers to a logical conclusion that results from a sequence of events, but beware the temptation to start with the story itself without first giving the reader reason to continue reading. Unless you are writing a novel, a story is useful only to illustrate or lead to some point or conclusion. If someone has to read paragraph after paragraph or page after page to get to that point, he may lose interest before you get around to the meaning of the story.

When the conclusion of a story is the main idea you wish to transfer, that conclusion should therefore be stated as the claim of the letter—*before* the story. The conclusion can be restated afterwards if the story is long, but placing the claim up front is the best way of ensuring readability in any letter. Look again at the memo about the sales call on Shipner Motors. Cover up the opening sentence and notice how mundane the letter seems until you get near the end.

With that sentence in place, however, the memo generates excitement from the beginning. Followed by a "one thing leads to another" backup, the opening claim teases and compels us to read until the details behind the large order are explained.

Never Let Go

As pointed out in chapter 7, reader attention is not something you merely must get. You must also keep reader attention. Accordingly, every claim, every back up, and every call for action has to be attention-getting.

The need to achieve a stranglehold on attention is greatest under two circumstances:

- when what you write is unsolicited and unexpected by a reader who doesn't know you and has no preference as to whether to communicate with you, with someone else, or with no one

- when what you write has been solicited by the reader but under conditions in which others have been motivated to compete with you

The two letter types that best meet these criteria are sale promotion letters and job application letters, both of which can be difficult to write when you have a lot at stake.

The example below is typical of what can be done with headlines to maintain attention throughout a sales letter. The job application letter, however, uses vertical lists to make certain that attention is never lost.

Sales Letter. Competing with a zillion other pieces of mail, an unsolicited sales letter must go all out to attract and capture reader attention. Notice how the product name is restated over and over again. Advertising a name is the exception to the repetition rules; repeating is the best way to advertise.

Dear Ms. Pointe:

Our new Model 6 Hyphenator will dramatically and economically increase the efficiency of your word-processing personnel and equipment.

Faster Typing. Up to 35 percent faster, according to independent tests. With the Model 6 Hyphenator, there's no need to stop to figure out how to handle word breaks at a right-hand margin, no need to consult a dictionary, and no need to hit the return button. Simply set your margins, type in the words, and the Hyphenator does the rest.

Self-Checking. The entire contents of Herman's New University Dictionary—237,000 words—are built in to the Hyphenator's memory. At the push of a button, the Model 6 Hyphenator will automatically scan all words and flash those that should be corrected. Even then, you don't have to stop to look up the right spelling; it is shown to you on the screen.

<u>Lay Out Letters Any Way You Want</u>
    –Single to triple spacing in half-space increments
    –8, 10, 12, or 15 letters to the inch
    –Proportional spacing on command
    –Single or double columns

<u>Four-Way Margins</u>. Not only does the Model 6 Hyphenator provide right and left justification, but it also offers our unique "bottomguard" system that allows you to set top and bottom margins and tells you how many lines you have left on a page.

<u>Universal Software</u>. Formatted to work with any ASCII-compatible equipment, the Model 6 Hyphenator is compatible with virtually any personal or business computer.

Judged by *Wordsmith* magazine to be the "most significant word-processing breakthrough in thirty years," the Model 6 Hyphenator is available for the low introductory price of only $189, and your money will be refunded in full if for any reason you are not satisfied within 30 days.

To get your Model 6 Hyphenator, fill in and mail the enclosed postpaid reply card. Should you prefer, call us toll-free at 800–555–3456.

We look forward to serving your word-processing needs.

Very truly yours,

Job Application Letter. Bosses are conservative in hiring decisions, and headlines might be too garish for their tastes. Tailoring the image to the need, someone seeking employment must give a "strictly business" impression, particularly when responding to "box number" ads that do not identify who the employer is.

For avoiding negatives while stressing strengths, vertical lists are a good way to draw attention to positives without giving a flashy appearance.

Dear Sir:

Since graduating from Sterling University with a degree in Industrial Journalism and Fine Arts, I have had more than ten-years' experience in high technology advertising and product literature design.

– Graphic Artist, Simtronics, Inc. Computer memories.

Responsible for advertising and brochure layouts, technical manual organization, and trade show displays.

- Advertising Manager, Datatek, Inc. Fully responsible for 5 writers, 2 graphic artists, and 2 secretaries. Formulated and implemented advertising and publicity plans and programs for 16 VHF and UHF transmitter product lines.

- Joined MicroLogic Industries Inc. five years ago as Advertising Manager. Promoted after 1 year to current position—Director of Communications. Responsible for all corporate publications, promotions, and advertising. In charge of staff of 12 and a budget in excess of 3 million dollars.

The following are my accomplishments applicable to your needs:

- Designed, wrote and negotiated printing for product literature, technical manuals, annual reports, proposals, and direct mail letters

- Created advertisements that won *HI-TEC* magazine's "Ad of the year" award on two occasions

- Author of "Add to your Ad" published last year by Von Slifer Press

- Adjunct Professor of Advertising, Rockleigh College

Although currently employed, I am interested in learning more about your operation, and I would welcome the opportunity to meet with you to further discuss how we might become associated on a mutually beneficial basis. Please let me know when such a meeting can be scheduled at your earliest convenience.

Very truly yours,

Getting in the Door

One of the most difficult objectives to achieve is to get an appointment with someone who doesn't know you and hasn't requested a meeting with you. Sometimes, the best way to obtain such an appointment is to force the reader into a corner by saying that you will be nearby his office at a specific time. This is what the following letter does as a follow-up to a previous letter which drew no response:

> Re: My letter to you of September 7
>
> Dear Mr. Jerome:
>
> During the week of November 22, I have to travel through Houston on other business, and I could easily adjust my schedule so we could meet then, at a time of your convenience.
>
> Given just a few minutes of your time, I could show you some of the graphics and copy that have made our advertising programs the preferred choice of an increasing list of industrial corporations, whose needs cover the gamut of business to business promotional communications.
>
> To confirm a time for our meeting, I will call your office on November 9. Should you be unable to talk with me then, please let your secretary know when such a meeting could best fit into your schedule.
>
> I look forward to seeing you the week of the 22nd.

Being somewhat specific about time gives the reader something both concrete and flexible. Saying that you'll be in the area has two benefits: it implies that you have other customers whose geographic interests are similar, and it allows the reader to not feel guilty about making you travel on sheer speculation. By then asking only that a secretary be given information to convey to you, the letter makes responding as easy as possible.

Calling for Action

Every call for action should be consistent with the tone and content of the letter it ends. Here's a letter as written before the call for action is written in:

> We have a major problem with the new computer.
>
> All programs written before last Friday have been erased. This

happened yesterday when several outside power lines were downed in a storm. When our electricity went out, everything in computer memory was erased due to the instantaneous power drain.

Fortunately, our backup memory on the old computer will help us re-create payroll and inventory files. Engineering programs, however, were never input on the old computer and have to be reinput from notes. Unless we are on-line within the next five days, our design activities will be forced to come to a halt.

This cannot be done while continuing to perform current work on time, and any slippage in existing production rates will reduce monthly shipments by at least 40 percent.

So far, so good. The letter attracts attention, makes the claim of program erasures and explains the claim along with its ramifications. At this point, the reader would expect a call to immediate action.

But suppose the letter ended by saying, "Let's review this matter at our meeting next week."

What a letdown! With that kind of ending, the writer is expressing a call for action that is inconsistent with the catastrophe just depicted.

Equally bad would be an ending that says, "Please let me know what you think we should do."

That isn't a call for action; it's an admission of ignorance. It also is inconsistent with the urgency described in the earlier paragraphs. What idea is being transferred here? That the writer has no idea of what to do?

Don't ever communicate such an idea, even if it is true. Give the reader something concrete to go on:

To resolve this situation, I have authorized double shifts and weekend hours for all engineering and programming personnel for the next ten days. In addition, I have hired three temporary computer operators through the middle of next week.

These steps will allow us to meet shipping schedules and to continue our design work without interruption.

You can present these solutions as suggestions and ask approval to proceed, but if you must have such approval, don't write—call.

Writing would be inconsistent with the time pressures conveyed in the earlier paragraphs.

Assuming that you can take action on your own and write, however, close by telling the reader what he wants to hear; that he still has some influence over how the problem is resolved: "If you have any additional suggestions or comments, please advise."

In the event that you must call for action in the midst of a letter, remember to start the cycle over again. Justify continuing by making a new claim, by backing that claim up as required, and by calling for action anew.

> Accordingly, we have decided to abandon the experiment.
>
> Our board of directors, however, has requested that we continue a low level of research on the mathematical solutions you suggested. That research will be initiated next month after I return from vacation.
>
> Please let me know if you have any preference as to our using the analogue approach or the digital system you originally recommended.

Properly used, a call for action can even be placed at the beginning of a letter. A command will always get a reader's attention. Such an opening always, however, must be followed up by an ending that reiterates or reinforces what you want to happen next.

Were you a dictatorial boss, you could start with a call for action that would be sure to attract a reader's attention: "Be in my office at 9:00 A.M. next Monday."

Upon reading such a sentence, people will naturally read further to find out what the meeting is about, and what the consequences might be for not attending. That opening therefore needs backup justification:

> Our warehouse space rental contract expires in ten days and we must establish accurate plans so that the new contract adequately meets our future needs.

With a memo this short, the message is quite clear, and only a first-class dummy would not see the urgency in attending. Perhaps a closing call for action is not necessary.

Then again, perhaps the moon is made of green cheese. Always close with a separate call for action, making certain that it narrowly focuses on what you want to happen next. Suppose, for example, that some readers have what they consider to be other high priority commitments next Monday. In that case, call for action in a way that clearly communicates the importance with which you view the meeting: "Your attendance at this meeting is mandatory; please clear your schedule of any conflicts."

But even that may not be enough. Are attendees supposed to just show up, or will they be expected to arrive with detailed forecasts from which warehouse space needs can be established? Or, do you want them to send in those forecasts in advance so that you can study them before the meeting? If so, you might want to say, "Also, send your space projections to me in time to arrive no later than Friday morning so that I can study them prior to the meeting."

Starting with a statement of what must be done, and proceeding through an explanation of why, the memo now gives complete details on what is expected. Let's add a "you and me" close and see what the assembled message looks like in total:

> Be at my office at 9:00 A.M. next Monday.
>
> Our warehouse space rental contract expires in ten days and we must establish accurate plans so that the new contract adequately meets our future needs.
>
> Your attendance at this meeting is mandatory, so clear your schedule of any conflicts. Also, send your space projections to me in time to arrive no later than Friday morning so that I can study them prior to the meeting.
>
> I look forward to seeing you on Monday.

Now, not only do the last two paragraphs call for action, but the final paragraph returns reader thinking to the original idea of being at the meeting. Also, the ending is personalized, giving each reader the added incentive of meeting an instinctive need to further associate in person with you. Alternatively, the personalized ending may appear to them as an opportunity to make points with you by showing up and thereby benefiting by giving you a chance to meet your needs to control their actions, to associate with you, or both.

But when you close, close. One thing leads to another, and a call for action should lead directly to that action, as is the case with the following:

> I would welcome the opportunity to meet with you to further explore your needs and to answer any questions you may have. I will call your office next Tuesday to determine when such a meeting can be scheduled at your earliest convenience.

The end of a letter should make the reader think not about your claim, not about your argument, and not about some postscript, but about what will happen next. Following a call for action, a *brief* personalized ending won't hurt, and a simple statement such as, "We look forward to your early favorable response," is OK, but don't stretch it out and don't force the reader to detour or look backward. Say what you want in the body of a letter; say it as powerfully, directly, and emphatically as you can, and sign off.

Efficient Use of Letter Space

Do whatever you can to compress all letters and memos onto one side of a sheet of standard-size letterhead paper. When a complete message is on one page, it can be read at a glance and quickly digested. Multipage letters, on the other hand, are less likely to have high readability and less likely to attract reader interest.

But getting everything on one page isn't always possible, so when two or more pages are required, you have to do everything possible with headlines, highlighting, vertical lists, and other techniques to make sure that reader interest is maintained.

An important part of restricting letters to one page is intense editing, a subject we will discuss in chapter 10. Of equal importance in many instances, however, are smart letter design practices starting with the way a letterhead is sized and placed.

As pointed out on page 92, there are good reasons for not putting your name on an envelope. On a letter within, no such reasons exist; a letter must announce who is doing the writing.

But that doesn't mean that a quarter of the page has to be taken up with the letterhead—that portion of the letter that identifies the name, address, and telephone number of the writer. Letterheads should be large enough to read without difficulty, yet small enough so that they do not excessively tie up space that could otherwise be used for text.

"Excessively," however, can not be defined without looking at the specifics of a letter on its own merits. A more meaningful measure of letterhead size is therefore obtained by asking yourself how small your letterhead can be while remaining bold and easily readable. The answer is that the bottom of your letterhead should be no more than 1 to 1½ inches from the top of the sheet.

A large corporate logo can't be jammed into that space, but personal or corporate name, address, and telephone number can fit quite nicely. For business stationery, logo height can be up to ¾ of an inch and still fit in the 1½-inch limit. Equivalent to the height of 5 lines of typewritten text, a logo that high is more than noticeable enough.

The following are representative examples of space-conscious letterhead designs:

William A. Jones ★ 123 Fourth Street New City, PA 23456
555–345–6789

JOULE PUBLICATIONS ★ 567 MAIN STREET
OGDEN, NJ 87654 ★ 212–976–1212
Technical manuals   Jackson P. Joule
                                    President

At your discretion, you can go to larger letterheads and, like many people, you can take up more than the 1½ inch recommended here. You will find, however, that for longer letters a large letterhead may on occasion force you to a second page that contains nothing more than a final sentence followed by your sign-off and signature. What a waste! Put the letterhead on one line, follow the design recommendations shown below, edit with a vengeance, and in many instances you'll get on one page what otherwise would require two pages.

After putting your letterhead in its place, center letters on the page as best you can. If this means two or three drafts, so what? A five-line memo looks funny when jammed up to the top of a full-size sheet of stationery. If you find yourself writing a lot of short memos or letters, get a supply of smaller-size letterheads—virtually every printer has an assortment of choices.

More than likely, however, more problems may crop up with regard to letters that seem to be too long to fit on one page. Often, such letters *can* fit on one page if space is intelligently used. This means using as much of the page as possible for text.

To make the most of available space, start at the top and begin typing three lines down from the bottom of the letterhead. Type in the name and address of the reader, leave a blank space, type in your salutation, leave another blank space and begin the text. Use a narrow margin of no more than five to ten spaces from the left edge of the sheet. On the right edge, do not hesitate to use a margin of as little as five spaces.

The date of a letter is often shown above the recipient's name and address, but if you need the space, put the date to the right of (and on the same line as) the reader's name. This saves at least 2 vertical spaces that would be virtually wasted if used only for date.

For the typing itself additional space efficiency can be gained by using what is called elite type, which prints 12 characters to the inch as opposed to pica type, which prints only 10 characters to the inch. An additional 2 characters per inch may not seem like a lot, but it is. Twelve over ten is 20 percent, which is equivalent to as many as six lines of type to the page, often more than enough to make the difference as to whether a message can fit on one page.

The foregoing space usage suggestions are illustrated next:

David H. Alan ★ 987 Sixth Avenue
Monsey, NY 10952 ★ 909–123–4567

Ms. Ann Mallard   November 6, 1988
660A Livingston Drive
San Diego, CA 41414

Dear Ann:

I have located all of the information you have requested.
The problem with your earlier research efforts was that the
Bolivian government had misunderstood your intentions.

At the end of the letter, leave a blank line before your signoff (two blank lines if you have the space) and four blank lines for your signature. If your name is in the letterhead, don't bother to type it in again beneath your signature. To avoid looking too jammed up, put nothing closer than an inch from the lower edge of the sheet. The bottom of a letter should look something like:

I look forward to seeing you again next Sunday.

Best regards,

Form Letters

When you do have to send the same letter to many readers, you'll do better by addressing each letter individually. This is most effectively done by typing each letter individually, but that means a great deal of work if more than a handful of readers are involved.

Word processors can individually type and address hundreds of letters, but the equipment to do that is expensive and word-processing service firms may charge more than you can afford. If more than several dozen letters are involved, however, word processing is the most practical way to personalize a quantity of letters.

For smaller quantities, however, another tact can be taken by using a typewriter that will accept the right kind of ribbon. Do not use a nylon ribbon; they last long, but only because they are designed to be used over and over again. As a result of extended use, however, nylon ribbons give dark impressions when new and increasingly lighter impressions as they are used.

A carbon film ribbon, on the other hand, is designed to give a crisper, sharper impression than a nylon ribbon. In addition, carbon ribbons are used only once; they do not rewind. When one is used up, it stops operating and a new ribbon must be inserted. Material typed on a film ribbon *always* has the same darkness as other material typed at any other time by that same film ribbon (or any other film ribbon from the same manufacturer).

Why worry about matching darkness? Because letters can be offset-printed to precisely match type darkness. Using a carbon film ribbon, type your letters leaving space for date, recipient name and address, and salutation. Then have the letter printed to match darkness, put each copy back into your typewriter, align and fill in the missing information using a carbon film ribbon. Even if that information is added weeks later, the lettering will all look the same.

Do not use a copy machine; most will not provide a good enough copy for this purpose and unless you happen to have access to a good enough photocopier, what you have done will be obvious. Some copiers also do not duplicate size precisely and even a 2 percent reduction will make alignment difficult or impossible.

In the event that you do not have access to a typewriter that accepts a carbon film ribbon, use what you have, but put in a new nylon ribbon when typing the text, and another new ribbon when the printed copies are worked on. Otherwise, the results will not look good.

With quality offset printing, careful alignment, and reliance on carbon film ribbons, on the other hand, letters will look individually prepared and the text will appear to have been typed at the same time as the material that was inserted later. Only by turning the sheet over will a reader be able to see that only the inserted information caused indentations in the paper. If you do a good job, however, no one will look back there.

Offset printing is available for approximately $10 to $15 per 100 copies at virtually any printshop. When you take work to a printer, insist on a perfect darkness match and refuse the work if that match is not provided.

Signing

John Hancock has a unique role in history because he knew that a bold signature stands out; it implies that you stand behind your words. A personalized signature says that you were willing to take the time to personally check and sign the letter. Such a signature tells the reader that he is not communicating with a word processor or copy machine, but with a bona fide human being who is making a definitive statement.

Individualized signing should be done even with several hundred letters; that may seem like a lot of work, but a couple of hours spent on signing can be well worth your while. If multiple signing is not feasible, have your signature printed in blue ink to stand out. Again, use a felt-tipped original and sign boldly.

However you sign a letter to be printed, don't sign on the letter itself. Put your signature several times on a sheet of plain white paper, and select with your printer the one that looks best. He can easily put that one in place.

Do It with Class

Good-looking stationery is a must for creating a professional image. It isn't expensive; 500 sheets of typeset letterhead, complete with that many printed envelopes, costs as little as $40 to $50. Printed on what is known as 25-percent rag content bond paper, your letterhead can be as professional as anyone elses.

Use white paper. Off-color material may draw attention, but it is also difficult to correct. Besides, nothing is more businesslike than plain white bond.

And don't just buy the paper and type your letterhead on. Typesetting itself, unless you get ripped off, should be no more than $10 to $20.

Aren't your communications objectives worth at least that much?

9

ANYTHING LONGER

Let's define a letter or memo as having a length of no more than a page or two. Anything that short can be given a great deal of readability simply by following the *ACBC* format described in chapter 8.

Longer documents are not that easy to deal with. Many of them are poorly written, difficult to follow, and all but impossible to use in terms of locating specific information. As a result, they all too often have excellent usefulness only as an alternative to sleeping pills.

Long documents can be effectively written in letter form, but only in the event that the reader has a strong interest in the topic and the writer's views coupled with a definite professional or personal relationship with the writer. Otherwise, anything longer than two or three pages can be given more strength by foregoing the "Dear Mr. Smith" type of opening and starting with a formal title page followed by logically sequenced and attractively head-lined text.

For anything longer than about four to six pages, you'll need a title page, headlined subdivisions, an easy-to-follow sequence, *and* a table of contents that identifies where each subdivision can be found. In addition, an introduction may be necessary to provide pertinent background information.

When more than ten pages are involved, even more work is necessary. To insure that readers are sufficiently motivated to read your version of the gospel, precede the text with a brief (one page or less) synopsis that summarizes objectives and contents while indicating the key points, results, or conclusions made on the pages to follow.

If you need fifty pages, a hundred pages, or several hundred pages, on the other hand, you'd better add a comprehensive, cross-referenced alphabetical index.

Getting people to read every word of a one-page letter is difficult, but motivating them to read every word of a ten-page report or proposal is next to impossible. The safe approach is to assume that they will *not* read every word.

But they *will* read those sections and words that—

- stand out, catch their eyes and command their attention;
- are easy to comprehend at a glance, such as titles, short synopses, descriptive headlines, and capsulized tables of contents.

Your job is to make sure that people can't possibly miss the essence of your message even if they do not read every word you write. This means that the longer your document, the more you'll have to be prepared to use the full gamut of readability tactics described in chapter 7: lists, tables, variations, positioning, sequence, tabulations, graphics, underlining, and attention-getting headlines.

Those tactics, combined with the *ACBC* format and with the guidelines presented in this chapter, will help you to write effective documents of any length.

Titling

To draw out reader interest in anything longer than a page or two, a title page never hurts. Title pages help to create attention by boldly announcing reports, proposals, and manuals in what will be seen as a professional manner.

A title page should contain five elements:

1. Identification of Document Type. Spell out what kind of a document follows. Is it a cost proposal, technical proposal, instruction manual, preliminary report, or

final report? If not, what is it? For quarterly reports or other documents covering a particular time span, that span should be identified. Remember to use a title that attracts attention (see page 99).

2. Identification of Subject Matter. As appropriate to each situation, the title page should refer to information such as program name and number, a reader's RFP (request for proposal) number and date, equipment name, type, and model number.

In the event that you do not know the names of the people to whom a document should be addressed within an organization, subject matter identification will make sure that what you have written gets into the right hands.

3. Name of Writer. When a document is prepared on behalf of a company or organization, its name and address should be clearly shown.

Most readers, however, find communicating with real people more inviting than hearing from corporations or other impersonal entities. So show your name and title, and sign the document boldly on the title page itself—don't make the reader go through a stack of pages to find out who you are.

Better yet, have two people sign: a specialist or department head who prepared the document; and that person's boss, who by signing signifies a high level of approval.

4. The Submittal Date.

5. The Name and Address of the Recipient. This step allows you to pay homage to the reader by printing his name in bold lettering, indicating that what follows has been prepared specifically for one reader or the organization in which he works.

If the material is likely to have several readers, organization name alone is adequate as long as subject matter has been identified. Reports, proposals, and manuals are not personally aimed as are letters, so individualized recipient naming is unlikely to detract from readability.

Should your document be unsolicited and unexpected, however, using an individual's name will not only help to generate a good first impression, it will also insure delivery to the right person.

Does this all seem too formal? You can always use a cover letter for additional personalizing. A sample title page is shown on page 149. See also the cover letter on page 152.

Tabulating Contents

A table of contents is the reader's primary means for determining how a document is organized, what the major subdivisions are, and where they can be found. If no alphabetical index has been prepared, a table of contents is the reader's only means (short of reading the whole thing) of determining what's inside. So make sure that tables of contents are complete and have entries that will be clear to your intended readers. If you have neither the time nor the energy to prepare a good table of contents, your readers cannot be expected to have the time or energy to struggle through a pile of pages to find what they want.

Sample Title Page

August 23, 1987

Final Report

GAS CONTENT ANALYSIS
STACK NUMBER 6
OMAHA NAVAL BASE

REFERENCE: NAVRFQ 16–961

Prepared for:

NAVINTOM
Materiel Branch 4–23
U.S. Naval Shipyards
Omaha, NE 54321

Attn: Captain J. P. Yardarm

Prepared by:

_____

T. D. Jenkins,
Senior Engineer

Approved by:

_____

W. S. Lewis,
Vice-President,
Engineering

Gas Analysis Corporation
678 Ninth Street
Pikesville, MD 01234

A table of contents should list the name of each major sub-division (the headline calling out that subdivision in the text) and the page on which that subdivision starts. If subdivision headlines are sufficiently descriptive to be fully understandable, that's all you may need, but if not, each entry in the table should be followed by a descriptive sentence or two. For an example of how this can be done, look at the table of contents in the front of this book.

Another option is to list secondary as well as main subdivisions. An instruction manual on a complex electronic instrument, for example, could contain details on how to operate many different controls for many different purposes. Unless each detail can be readily located, the manual's usefulness will be limited. A table of contents with subdivision listings would in part say:

For documents that must be separated into more than one volume, the table of contents should be repeated in each volume, with each item location noted by page number and volume number. One way to do this is to have separate pagination for each volume. A 47-page first volume, for instance, could have pages identified as I–1 through I–47. A 64-page second volume could then be numbered II–1 through II–64.

Synopses

As a *brief* summary of what a document contains, a synopsis provides readers with a capsulized condensation of what they are about to read.

A synopsis should *always* be a page or less in length. It can be on a page by itself immediately preceding the text, and it can be in the form of a cover letter preceding the document. If room is available, you can even put it on the title page. Publishers, to draw attention to a book, often put synopses right on the cover or jacket.

With a synopsis, readers are given a distillation of a report so that without having to read the entire document, they can see what it contains in terms of topics, key results, conclusions, and what will or should happen next.

Synopsis

Three hundred sunglass wearers were surveyed for their reactions to the price, comfort, glare-resistance, and style of UltraRay lenses and frames.

Reactions were favorable to all factors except glare resistance. More than eighty percent said that our lenses did an excellent job of protecting their eyes, but that this was a plus only in bright sunlight. At other times, they found the lenses too dark to see through.

They suggested that we sacrifice some glare resistance to allow the lenses to be used in a broader variety of light levels.

The next phase of the program—testing with lenses that pass more light—has started and will be concluded in thirty days.

A synopsis need not necessarily provide backup details, but it must say just enough to impart to readers the essence of what was done and what is said in the text that follows.

But not all documents involve objectives, methods, and results. An instruction manual, for example, would require a synopsis that says, "Here's what this manual contains," by summarizing the scope rather than results.

Synopsis

Instructions are provided for installing and operating the IRF Model 4563 electric dust pan on carpeted floors.

In addition to step-by-step setup and usage instructions, the manual contains a troubleshooting guide and detailed routine maintenance instructions.

For documents that you want to be read in their entirety, synopses should act as an appetite-whetter, summarizing contents in such a way that people are compelled to read further. This is often achieved with proposals by putting the synopsis in the form of a cover letter that also serves to personalize and tailor the message.

> Dear Ms. Stewart:
>
> In accordance with your request of November 6, enclosed is our proposal for your new boiler.
>
> Note that we shall meet your specifications without exception, and that our delivery shall be well within your schedule limitations. More importantly, note that we have found a way to do the job at thirty percent below your budget.
>
> Should you have any questions, please call me at any time. Otherwise, we look forward to your early favorable response.

How did the cost come in that low? Ms. Stewart will have to read the proposal to find out.

Setting the Stage

Synopses summarize, but introductions explain.

An introductory section is required when—

- the combination of title page and synopsis cannot describe a document well enough so that readers will fully understand and appreciate its scope and limitations;

- more personalizing is appropriate than could be otherwise achieved;

- a complete understanding of the document's meaning requires historical background information;

- readers would otherwise not know why the document was written, why it was sent to them, or both.

Introductions are stage-setters. A plan for a new product, for example, might be introduced with a description of how the product is necessary to meet marketplace needs prompted by products offered by competitors, as well as a tabular analysis of what those competitors offer.

Like synopses, introductions can be located in front of the text or built into cover letters. Aside from serving as a synopsis, the cover letter on page 152 acts as an introduction by telling Ms. Stewart why the proposal was written and by identifying the prior request to which the proposal is responding. It also personalizes the proposal to her needs.

When no cover letter is used, there are two ways that an introduction can be included within the text:

1. to put the introduction on a page by itself; this way, you provide "something for everybody" by allowing people who don't need the introduction to easily skip it and go right on to the main body of the document

2. to use the introduction as the first section in the text; this approach is better when you want to make certain that the introductory material is read

Unfortunately, many people write introductions that have information not needed for readability. Typical examples are acknowledgments made to those individuals who helped the writer in researching, typing, writing or editing. We in turn are conditioned to finding that reading such an introduction is a waste of our time. So what do we do? We skip it.

To prevent that from happening, mention acknowledgments separately under a section so titled and located at the beginning or end of the document. For introductory material that readers *must* see to fully understand what you are talking about, put it at the beginning, but don't give it a dull or dry name like "Introduction" or "Program history."

Draw those readers in with an eye-catching "The Problem with Prior Results."

On page 151, you read a synopsis for an instruction manual on an electric dust pan. That same manual, to communicate the writer's position on the scope of the manual, might say:

> *WARNING*
> The IRF Model 4563 electric dust pan has been designed for home use on dry floors. The instructions contained herein do not apply to operation in industrial environments or wet environments.
> Should you have such applications for an electric dust pan, contact our factory for information on our Models 4573, 4583, and 4595.

That'll catch reader eyes.

Organization

When written material is short and can be read at a glance, it lends itself to "hit-and-run" communication tactics that within seconds blitz us with a message ending with a direct, "Here's what's next" ending. That is what the *ACBC* format does with letters and memos.

By itself, however, *ACBC* generates a slam-bang impact only when *A, C, B,* and *C* can be seen at a glance. As a message gets longer and longer, its totality cannot be read in a few seconds and *ACBC* will not work by itself; it must be augmented by properly sequenced and headlined subdivisions, with text highlighted as required to make key points stand out.

Long documents should open with a multiple of attention-getters; before people will start tackling multiple pages, they have to be attracted by a combination of title page, synopsis, table of contents, and introduction.

Text organization can then follow in virtually any "one thing leads to another" sequence as long as it will seem logical and complete to the reader. Individual sections can be written in a "get attention, make a claim and back it up" sequence, but section-to-section organization must be designed to suit the type and purpose of the document.

There are so many long document types and purposes that one organizational sequence cannot be used for all applications, but the following guidelines can be adapted to virtually all needs.

Instruction Manuals

The objective of an instruction manual is to show readers how some device should be operated, installed or fixed. Such a manual should contain four main sections:

1. A functions subdivision that describes the purpose of every dial, button, switch, lever, or control mechanism on the device.

   One way to do this is to use photographs surrounded by clusters of text to describe a different aspect of the device. The object here is to say something like, "Here's what happens when you push this button," or "Here's what this dial is for."

   Instead of (or in addition to) the captioned picture, text subdivisions can be established for each item described.

2. An applications section can be written for each purpose for which the device being explained was intended.

   Rather than talking about one dial or button at a time, this part of the manual should show how controls are used in concert to achieve some clearly defined objective.

   Do not be afraid to repeat photographs or figures here. If each purpose requires pushing a different combination of buttons on an instruction panel, show the panel each time, pointing out the proper buttons to be used.

3. A trouble-shooting section that lists, identifies and provides solutions for typical operating problems, while pointing out any areas that require expert repairs.

4. A routine maintenance section that enumerates and describes steps the reader can and should take in the way of preventive maintenance.

Instruction manuals need not be formatted according to *ACBC*, but they must be organized in such a way that readers can easily find what they want about any covered aspect of the device about which the manual was written.

Instruction manuals are most useful when the applications section is written as a series of step-by-step lists that detail operating procedures in a logical sequence. The prospect of pulling operating sequence out of long paragraphs is about as inviting as that of having teeth pulled without an anesthetic.

Remember to write on only one subject at a time. Knowing how something works—the theory behind its design—is *not* necessary to become proficient in how to operate it. The objective of an instruction manual is to provide enough information so that readers can use a particular device. Unless including the design theory helps to meet that objective, stick to how the device can be used and stay away from why it works the way it does.

Want to write about design theory? Fine, but don't do it in the midst of an instruction manual. Use a report.

An old adage in writing says that we should write on subjects with which we are most familiar. To a point, that's good advice, but that point does not extend into the realm of instruction manuals.

The guy who invented or designed a machine is typically the *last* person who should write the instruction manual on it. When you are the world's authority on a particular device, you may be able to objectively write about how it works, but chances are, you'll not be able to adequately anticipate and answer all the questions that may arise on its operating procedure.

This may not be a problem with simple equipment or with devices readers have used before, but technological hardware is another story. Computers and other hi-tech equipment are notorious for including manuals that tend to be useless because of their inadequate instructions.

If possible, instruction manuals should therefore be written by people who have no previous contact with the device. They'll be more likely to ask all the "stupid" questions a typical reader might ask, and as a result the manuals they write will be more useful.

Reports

What Was. The most common type of reports are historical records. To be effective, "what was" reports should convey information in five main sections, sequenced as follows:

1. What happened?
2. When, where, why, and how it happened, who was involved, and how much it cost?
3. How does it compare to what was expected?
4. What does it mean?
5. What will or should happen next?

In addition to "what was" reports, you may also have occasion to write "what is" reports and "what will be" reports.

What Is. This type of report describes concepts or facts. Organization is again in five main sections. A typical example is:

1. What is the concept?
2. What incentives does it offer?
3. How does it work?
4. What (or what else) can it be used for?
5. What could be done to make it better?

"What is" reports are ideal to describe the theory behind that contraption about which you have written an instruction manual.

What Will Be. Sales or business forecasts fall into this category, which is similar to "what happened" reports except for tense:

1. What will happen?
2. When, where, why, and how it will happen, who will be involved, how much it will cost?
3. How will it compare to what we would like to have happen?

4.   What will it mean?

5.   What can or should we do about it?

All reports can effectively use the *ACBC* format. As just organized, they start with an attention-getting title page, synopsis, table of contents, and introduction; the text then begins with a claim, continues with backup explanatory sections, and concludes with a call to action.

Proposals

Proposals should also be subdivided into four sections, sequenced as follows and subdivided with appropriate headlines and text highlighting:

1.   What you propose, stated in terms of benefits to the reader. Come right out swinging with a direct statement of "Here's what we'll do for you and this is what you get out of it!" Pour on those incentives.

2.   How it works. Describe the approach to be used and show how logical it is.

3.   How reliable, durable, attractive, safe, and inexpensive it is. Point out how similar ideas have worked elsewhere with great success. Other subdivisions here include your "track record" of success as a supplier, the track record and capabilities of the people you'll have working on the project, and examples of instances in which what you propose will provide incentives the reader wants. If the reader has known specifications for whatever is being proposed, this section can also be used to show how you meet those specifications on an item-by-item basis.

4.   Call for action. Sell, sell, sell.

Don't forget to highlight strengths while sidestepping any potential weaknesses. If, for example, your proposal has an attractive price, make it stand out by putting it up front in a cover letter or synopsis. It should then also be stated in a clearly identified text subdivision and repeated again in the call for action, along with assurances that no incentives have to be sacrificed in order to take advantage of your attractive price.

A high price, on the other hand, will require justification. High prices can be inserted, without highlighting, in the middle of the text, but they cannot be completely sidestepped. What you *can* do is to justify your price in terms of the additional incentives you offer compared to others touting a lower price. What features does your widget have that the other guy doesn't have? Point them out in a "no negatives" manner.

Alternatively, perhaps a high price now means lower costs later on. Or maybe it means decreased energy expenses? Lower labor costs? Less in the way of long-term maintenance? Highlight those facts and imply that, "When you examine all this information, my price is actually quite low."

When needed, a strong price justification story should have its own section in a proposal. Titled something like
"TWENTY-PERCENT ENERGY SAVINGS,"
or
"CUTTING LABOR COSTS IN HALF,"
that section need not say anything about a high initial price unless you want to include long-term cost comparisons that strengthen your arguments.

Plans

Many people fail to succeed at their jobs or businesses simply because they do not know how to write an effective business plan. There's a big difference between having a workable plan and making that plan look attractive to readers whose approval, financing, or cooperation you need to go ahead on a project.

Assuming that you do in fact have a good plan, sequence it into seven main sections:

1. Plan Objectives Stated in Terms of Reader Benefits. This is the place to describe anticipated end results and to highlight how those results translate to reader incentives.

2. Methods of Accomplishment. This section is a description of:
   —how the stated objectives will be met on a step-by-step basis;
   —who will do what for each step;
   —where and when each step will occur;
   —how much each step will cost;
   —when each step will be reported.
   A proposal's methods of accomplishment can be written up in paragraph form and in tabular form for easy reading.

3. Resource Analysis. Funding, manpower, equipment, and facilities necessary to do the job compared to that which is currently available. Methods for obtaining required resources are detailed in this section. This is where you say, "Here's what it takes to make it happen."

4. Contingencies. This section is great for convincing people that you're not trying to con them. Here you point out everything that could realistically be expected to go wrong, in each case providing a backup plan indicating how you would compensate if problems cropped up.
   Your intention here is to give the impression of being prudent. "Sure, there may be problems, but there will not be *unforeseen* problems."

5. Plan Reliability. This section is used to convince readers that the proposed method of accomplishment is logical and feasible, that resources can be made available if the plan is approved, that the schedule is realistic, and that all contingencies have been adequately considered.
   There should also be in this section a statement of

previous successes with the same idea or similar ideas, as well as mention of the successes and capabilities of the people who will be implementing the plan.

6. Return on Investment. Implementing the plan will cost money. If you have done your homework, however, you'll be able to show how that money will serve as an investment that will be returned by future savings in the form of incentives like greater productivity or decreased operating costs. Don't generalize; be as specific as possible.

7. Summary and Call for Action. Key incentives for plan approval are listed, reader benefits are summarized, and a schedule of start-up requirements are stressed to spur early go-ahead. The plan then ends with a call for action.

Plans can be viewed as tools to help you organize your activities, but in most instances, plans are much more than that. Usually, a plan is the written vehicle by which corporate management, bankers, partners, investors, or clients are persuaded to approve someone's scheme for a concerted course of action. As such, a planning document is a specific kind of proposal; its purpose is to sell.

Planning documents are constantly being updated and amended as the plans are enacted. In this regard, plans are "living"—over the course of time, they are revised through interim reports that communicate status as compared to planned milestones, and recommend how future portions of the plan should be changed to reflect knowledge learned to date. Plans should point out that progress reports will be so constructed and issued regularly according to a specific schedule.

Indexing

An alphabetical index is far more than an alphabetized table of contents. It is in alphabetical order, but not just for main sections; every topic, subtopic, and subsubtopic must be included. Since a given subject can go under different names, an index should list *all* such names, cross-referencing all names under which the same subject is listed. At the end of this book, for example, you will find entries for both "alphabetical index" and "indices," with the latter saying, "See alphabetical index" to find the pages on which the topic is discussed. *A Manual of Style* covers indexing procedures and techniques in great detail.

Many writers find indexing too much work, and many do a sloppy job of it, but they don't have to respond to what they have written. Upon finding that topics are hard to locate, many of their readers don't respond either.

Listing References

That's right—you have to go to another book to get detailed instructions on writing an alphabetical index. Were the same information to be repeated here, this chapter would lose focus because a disproportionate amount of space would be consumed on a topic only peripheral to the main subject of transferring ideas in print.

Aside from serving to back up the validity of your claims and to help shorten the text by keeping it sharply focused, references are often used merely to provide people with additional reading material on related subjects.

You can include references in many ways: separately or in combination; they can be mentioned within the text; they can be shown in footnotes; they can be listed on a table located before or after the text and clearly indicated in the table of contents. Again, *A Manual of Style* will help.

EDITING

To edit is to identify and correct any errors that might prevent a document from meeting its objectives. You can write whatever you want in a first draft, but unless what your reader sees is an error-free final draft, you're in trouble.

Mention editing to the average person and he will immediately come up with images of correcting grammatical, spelling, punctuation, or word usage mistakes. Certainly when one writes something like, "Jane Carstairs was elected yesterday as president of the world's largest manufacturers association," careful editing would identify that as written, the sentence is ambiguous. Does this sentence mean that only the world's largest manufacturers are in the association, or that her association is the largest one whose members are manufacturers? Depending on what the facts are, the sentence should be written as either, "Jane Carstairs was elected yesterday as president of the world's largest association of manufacturers," or "Jane Carstairs was elected yesterday as president of the association of the world's largest manufacturers."

This type of editing is done to make certain that ideas are stated in clear prose, free of ambiguities. The mere expression of ideas, however, is but one of several facets of communicating. To be comprehensive, editing cannot be limited to finding and fixing grammar and wording faults. Any mistakes that are counter-productive from an idea transfer standpoint must be located and revised as required in accordance with the previous nine chapters.

Complete editing means asking and addressing ten questions

whenever you write something:

1. Have I used the right words, spelling, punctuation, and grammar?
    Have I been clear? Will my reader interpret what I have said the way I want him to interpret it, or have I left in ambiguities? Are my sentences consistent with my purposes in both meaning and form?

2. Is it "all positives and no negatives"?
    Have I gone directly to the bottom line to avoid generating unanswered questions? Have I side-stepped or circumvented all negatives? Will I evoke hope and trust instead of fear and anger?

3. Is the writing lively and readable, or is it boring and repetitive?
    Will it get and maintain reader attention throughout?

4. Is it tailored to each reader as an individual?
    Will the reader feel that this was written specifically for his unique needs? Have I given each reader what he wants to see in print?

5. Are the right points appropriately highlighted?
    Or are they buried within the text and hard to find?

6. Have I offered enough of the right incentives?
    Will my reader have to ask, "What's in it for me?" or will the answer be provided with compelling force before the question is asked?

7. Is it logically organized and sequenced?
    Will my train of thought be obvious and easy to follow?

8. Does it look good?
    Will it give the impression of having been written by a knowledgeable professional or by a hack?

9. Is it sharply focused?
    Have I stayed on track or are there subjects here that might best be left out or discussed elsewhere?

10. Has all excess baggage been eliminated?
    Have I included anything that should be deleted or rewritten so as not to detract from the impact or readability I want?

Any time you come up with a "no" or "maybe" answer to any of these questions, you have probably committed a communications error.

Fix it!

These questions look at writing in two ways: for meaning and for "look at a glance" visual impact. This is the way readers will view it; first they will see overall appearance and what is highlighted, and then they will read the words.

Accordingly, do not expect to edit in one shot. Words, punctuation, and grammar can to some extent be corrected as you go along, but factors such as overall appearance, sequence, and highlighting can be examined only by standing back from word-by-word scrutiny and taking a "big picture" view of at least one page at a time.

Another reason for finalizing in stages is that the ten editing questions are interactive. Changes in response to one question may mean changes in the way other questions are answered. Revised wording to explain a point, for example, may position other wording so that it doesn't stand out and has to be moved to insure adequate readability.

Editing must be done from two points of view: yours and your reader's. Yours is easy, but are you objective enough to put yourself in the reader's shoes to accurately predict how *he* would answer the ten editing questions? If not, you probably will not meet your goals. Unless you are careful, your concentration will be more on what you want to say than it is on what the other guy wants to read.

Give yourself time to "shift gears" after writing. Go on to something else so that when you do come back to editing, you can do it with a fresh outlook. And be prepared to shift gears more than once; the further you get from the frame of mind you were in while writing, the closer you will get to being objective about editing.

Have Someone Else Proofread for You

That's *for* you—not instead of you. The ideal proofreader is someone who does not know what you're talking about and who has no strong stake in whether your ideas are transferred to readers. Such a person can concentrate on insuring the proper usage of words, spelling, punctuation, and grammar. He can also help to answer question 3 on liveliness, and question 8 on overall appearance.

Why someone who doesn't know the topic? Because a proofreader looking for meaning may have a hard time focusing on matters such as usage, appearance, or whether certain words are needlessly repeated. In your case, you cannot, being the author of a document, concentrate entirely on something as mundane as grammar—your primary outlook will be on winning arguments, not on repairing dangling participles.

That's why you are probably your own worst proofreader If most of your work is typed by others, ask for their advice and demand that they not merely tell you that you are the greatest writer since Shakespeare. Suggest that they look for writing faults such as repetition. A "warts and all" critique from a third party today is a lot better than failing to communicate to your reader tomorrow.

After you get someone else to edit, do it yourself as a double check and do it again and then again to go over the readability, tailoring, sequence, "no negatives," and incentives factors that only you and your reader can meaningfully evaluate.

Take a Memo

Dictating has been touted as a way to make life easy for business people. Documents can be "written" anyplace: on airplanes, in your car on the way to work, or between holes on a golf course. It's easy—you have only to put in good batteries and a fresh tape, press the button and spout out what you have in mind. Your secretary can then make sure that all spelling and punctuation is correct. All you need do at that point is to check for typos and you're all done. Easy, isn't it?

No way. Dictating is an excellent way to make notes on information you don't want to forget and it is fine for short memos, but it is also a guaranteed way to give yourself a lot of editing headaches with anything longer than a couple of short paragraphs.

You cannot see the first draft of dictated material; it's on tape or in shorthand on a memo pad. As a result, you cannot see whether the right material is highlighted or buried in the text. If more than half a dozen paragraphs are involved, you may not even be able to visualize whether the overall effect has a logical sequence. Chances are, you may not be able to remember whether you have provided all the necessary reader incentives in a coherent manner. You also will not be able to tell whether your paragraphs are too short or too long.

Some people can do all this in their heads, but rarely can it be done well for a multifaceted full page letter and never can it be done well for anything longer. Dictating forces you to wait for a typed draft before doing any serious editing.

You'd be better off to type it yourself if you can. At the least, write out your first draft longhand. Either way, *see* what the whole thing looks like so that you can edit visual aspects as you struggle for the right words and grammar. *Then* dictate; you'll be in a much better position to use the initial rough draft as a basis for evaluating factors such as highlighting, paragraph length, and sequence.

No matter how competent your secretary may be, she cannot be expected to edit for incentives, tailoring, or proper sidestepping. You must do all that yourself, and dictating should never be allowed to con you into believing that it offers any communication shortcuts. All it offers is a quick way to get a first draft off your chest. Any work it saves in doing that, however, is usually more than compensated for in the form of additional editing required in subsequent drafts.

Get Rid of Excess Baggage

If you can effectively use the English language, and if you follow the advice already given in this book, you should be able to handle the first nine editing questions. The tenth is another matter.

What is excess baggage? Words or ideas that would or might evoke negatives, repeat what you have already said, distract by veering off into unrelated topics, or provide explanations the reader does not need.

Wording that falls into these categories should be eliminated or rewritten. On close examination, you will see that editing for excess baggage in essence serves as a backup for the editing questions about negatives, sharp focus, tailoring, and maximum readability.

Still another kind of excess baggage is wording that could be eliminated with no detrimental effect. Take another look at the previous sentence. Can you find a word that can be left out with no loss of meaning? Start at the beginning; why is the word *still* used? Other than to illustrate a point about nonessential terminology, the word serves no essential purpose. Also, how about changing ". . . why is the word *still* used?" to ". . . why is *still* used?" and while we're making progress, reducing ". . . illustrate a point about nonessential terminology. . . ." to ". . . illustrate non-essential terminology. . . ."

Anything missing with those words removed? Certainly no meaning is missing. Only excess baggage is missing; what started as a sixteen-word sentence was cut to thirteen words—a reduction of roughly 19 percent. That may not seem like a lot, but it is. Reduce everything that much and you will—

- cut as much as five to eight lines from a letter that previously took up a full page;
- reduce to one page a letter that previously had run five to eight lines on a second page;
- pare a fifty-page proposal down to just over forty pages;
- drop almost nineteen pages from a hundred-page report.

And all this can be done with no loss of meaning, no loss of incentives, no loss of readability, and no loss of motivational power.

Here's a few other excess baggage examples:

His performance was the best in the ~~entire~~ country. (*entire* adds nothing to the meaning.)

Bill ~~is a man who~~ knows what he wants. (If Bill is a woman, that's a different story.)

The message was broadcasted to all the ships ~~at sea~~. (Where else would the ships be?)

I don't know whether ~~or not~~ to go to Chicago next week. ("or not" adds nothing.)

We are ~~pretty~~ certain to enjoy the meeting. (*Certain* means "definite," or "for sure." *Pretty certain* means nothing.)

We tried the same ~~exact~~ approach last year. (superfluous.)

This is precisely the ~~same~~ conclusion we came to. (also superfluous.)

We have a ~~very~~ unique solution. (*Unique* means "one of a kind." *Very* adds nothing.)

Enclosed ~~herewith~~ is the report you requested. (Where else would the reader expect the report to be enclosed?)

Attached ~~hereto~~ is your receipt. (To what else might one expect it to be attached?)

Jim went to New York ~~in order~~ to close a big order. ("in order" can always be deleted from "in order to.")

The information was expressed in two ~~separate~~ documents. (Unless they were stapled together.)

This book contains many ~~different~~ tips on effective writing. (Certainly it would not contain many of the same tips.)

~~Please be advised that~~ We accept your offer. (Forget the useless introduction.)

Don't forget ~~the fact~~ that they have not yet paid us. ("the fact" can usually be deleted.)

~~Kindly~~ Fill in and mail the enclosed postpaid reply card. (Might the card otherwise be filled in angrily? Mailed angrily?)

Send your recommendations ~~to me~~ as soon as possible. (To whom else would they be sent?)

This ~~is a photograph that~~ shows our new building. (Readers would not
know that they were looking at a photograph?)
Although words can be cut ~~out~~, simple deletion is not always the answer.
(Would they be otherwise cut in?)

"Simple" is left in the last example because getting rid of excess
baggage often requires rewriting so that the result is grammatically
correct. Otherwise, the first editing question (on usage) could not
be properly answered. When, for instance, you see a word group
starting with "that is, . . ." "that are, . . ." "who is, . . ." or "who
are, . . ." look closely; you may be able to cut with a little
rewriting.

"I have a dog that is well-trained," can in this regard be
shortened to "I have a well-trained dog," while "Most people who
are from Paris speak in French," in shortened form, becomes,
"Most Parisians speak French."

"That is, . . ." and "who are, . . ." clauses do not always lend
themselves being rewritten in shortened form, but they should in
every instance be examined so that opportunities for cutting are not
missed.

Another example of "cut and rewrite" is a variation on a
sentence discussed earlier: "Enclosed please find the report you
requested." "Please find"? Will the report be difficult to locate?
The sentence is fine as is if you are conducting a scavenger hunt, but
if tight editing is your goal, get rid of the *please find* business and
replace it with an *is*.

Be Direct

Sentences embellished with useless or obvious "explanations" are
prime candidates for editing:

~~I am writing this letter to~~ Thank you for your generous contribution.
(Might the reader have suspected that someone else had written the
letter and signed your name? Would the reader otherwise think that
instead of your writing a letter that your brother-in-law was baking a
cake? Might the reader not realize that he was reading a letter?)

~~I would like to take this opportunity to extend my~~ Congratulations ~~to you~~ on your promotion.

(If you want to say something in writing, say it—don't just say that you would *like* to say it. Besides, whose congratulations would the reader assume you were extending—Marco Polo's? Or, would the reader have thought that congratulations were being extended to someone else?)

~~We are sorry to say that~~ Your application cannot be accepted.

(This is an often used (but inept) way of expressing bad news. Are you sorry that the reader's application cannot be accepted, or are you sorry that you have to be the one to say that it cannot be accepted? As originally written, the sentence expresses the latter option; who cares about your guilt feelings?

Should you wish to communicate regret, do it in another sentence and be clear about it.)

~~This next section was particularly difficult to write.~~ (Who cares?)

The most effective way to get an idea across is to highlight it as per chapter 6 and to hit the reader with it "right between the eyes" with no excess baggage and with explanations limited strictly to those which are necessary to go directly to his "bottom line" of understanding.

Design Sentences to Suit

The basic assumption made in this book is that you have already studied traditional grammar books and that you either know how to construct sentences or know when to consult an outside source to check for the right wording or puctuation.

What traditional grammar books don't tell you, however, is that writing a "proper" sentence does not necessarily insure that you will be communicating the right idea. To illustrate this point, assume that your objective is that someone attends a meeting in your office next Monday morning. Assume further that incentives are provided by the truckload, and that everything else appears to check out when evaluated against the ten editing questions: "Can you be here next Monday morning at 10:00 A.M.?"

Your intent may be understood, but this is weak motivation. Interpreted literally, the question merely asks the reader to get back to you with a "yes" or "no" answer. *But it doesn't ask him to be at the meeting*; it merely *implies* such a request.

Questions have two purposes: to solicit specific information ("Who wrote that report?") or to ask for a "yes" or "no." In the instance of your meeting next Monday, asking a question motivates action only if it is accompanied by a command: "Can you be here next Monday morning at 10:00 A.M.? Let me know by Thursday."

That's better, but what action is requested? Attending the meeting? No—answering the question.

Another way to express what you want is to make a statement: "I expect to see you at the meeting Monday morning at 9:00 A.M."

The sentence is fine from a grammatical standpoint, but it does nothing but express *your* hopes. Yes, if you are a dictatorial boss and your reader an employee, the implication may be clear, but the request is nevertheless indirect. The same goes for, "I would appreciate your being here Monday morning at 9:00 A.M."

Once again, a clear sentence expressing what you want, but again the reader has to "read between the lines" to get the full impact of what you are saying. Unless pleasing you is an incentive unto itself for your readers, you'll have to get more emphatic: "You must be here Monday morning at 9:00 A.M."

A "You must. . . ." sentence has more oomph than an "I would appreciate. . . ." sentence, but both still reflect writer viewpoint, not reader viewpoint. Sorry, but you'll have to find a still more emphatic way to get your point across.

That way is to be direct and specific. In the case of motivating for action, expressing what you want should be done with a command: "Be here Monday morning at 9:00 A.M."

Combined with adequately personalized incentives and good readability, commands put things out of the realm of your opinion, your needs, and your feelings, and directly in the realm of what must happen. You can't be more effective than that. Look closely and you'll see that the command also has the benefit of using fewer words than either the question or statement forms originally attempted. Does the command form seem too blunt for a particular reader? The sentence can be tailored to suit by adding just one word: "Please be here next Monday morning at 9:00 A.M."—Still fewer words than the original versions, and still more direct and emphatic.

Examples abound in which sentences must be rewritten to a form more consistent with their purpose. To get information, for example, one might say, "I need to know who you work with in Tokyo," or "I would appreciate your telling me who you work with in Tokyo."

Neither is as short or as direct as saying, "Tell me who you work with in Tokyo," or "Please tell me who you work with in Tokyo."

A question here would also be appropriate, but make sure you ask, "Who do you work with in Tokyo?" or "With whom do you work in Tokyo?"

Either question asks for information, but, "Can you tell me who you work with in Tokyo?" merely requests a "yes" or a "no."

Editing for sentence form is an important facet of written communications. Whatever your objective, take another look at chapter 2 and rewrite as required so that each sentence is expressed in the form best suited for the specific purpose you have in mind for it. Not only will doing so result in more effective idea transfer, but it will in many cases also eliminate still more excess baggage.

Grouping and Combining Ideas

To group and combine ideas, one has to know how to construct sentences. Discussing that aspect of writing is not within the scope of this book, but the following will show that combining two or three sentences can significantly reduce word count: "I did not have enough money for the transaction. Accordingly, I asked my secretary to have our bank transfer sufficient funds to a bank near my hotel. The transfer will be completed by Friday" is a thirty-four–word paragraph consisting of three sentences. Each of the sentences is well written, and each is clear, but so is this:

> Not having enough money for the transaction, I asked my secretary to have our bank transfer, by Friday, sufficient funds to a bank near my hotel.

Now the same information is expressed in only one sentence made up of only twenty-six words. That's a reduction of almost 24 percent!

"Our New England region consistently brings in a million dollars annually. In contrast, our west coast people never meet quotas," is another example of excessive wording. Once again, the meaning is clear, but one too many words has been used. The solution? Combine the two sentences into one:

> Our New England region consistently brings in a million dollars annually, but our west coast people never meet quotas.

Don't bother counting; the one sentence version uses 19 words as compared to 20 which were needed with two sentences.

In the first example, three sentences were combined by expressing the original first sentence as a participial phrase ("Not having enough money for the transaction"), by stating the third sentence as a prepositional phrase (by Friday), and by making those phrases part of what had originally been the second sentence.

The second example, however, combined ideas by using what is called a coordinating conjunction (but) to join what had previously been two sentences into one sentence consisting of two clauses. *But* means "in contrast" here, so one word and a comma took the place of two words and a period.

Phrases, clauses, and conjunctions may or may not achieve the word reductions just shown, but if you understand the jargon and can construct decent sentences, you'll find many opportunities to reduce word count.

Let the Experts Help You

This is *not* an "Everything you would ever want to know about. . . ." book. No one book contains *everything* about written communications. To alert you to what to look for when editing, however, this chapter has been designed to point out some of the more typical writing faults you may encounter. Additional information can be found in the books listed in the Bibliography. A more comprehensive review of editing, for example, can be found in *Edit Yourself*; aside from listing many more word-cutting examples than are shown here, it shows how to correct numerous grammatical errors.

For easy-to-read, yet excellent writing tips, try *The Elements of Style*. You'll benefit from its lists of dos and don'ts on writing style and grammar. *A Pocket Guide to Correct English, Essentials of English*, and *The Writer's Hotline Handbook*, on the other hand, delve into sentence construction in greater detail. Each of these four books contains alphabetized usage guides that will help you to avoid the pitfalls of commonly misused wording, as well as instructions on the use of punctuation for clarity in expressing ideas. *A Manual of Style*, on the other hand, will be useful not only in looking up accepted norms of punctuation, but also in areas such as knowing how to use numbers, abbreviations, and capitalization.

Do not forget, however, that unless your objective is to pass a test in English, you are writing to transfer ideas, not to blindly use rules. Never use any grammatical rules that interfere with your ability to communicate.

As an example, just about every writing guide will tell you to express yourself in the simplest terms possible. *Ear* is therefore preferable to *auditory organ* or *organ of hearing*. In writing about hearing, however, using *ear* on every line might hinder readability, so a longer synonym would not be harmful if used infrequently to eliminate repetition. For this reason, the next paragraph uses *develop a solid expertise* to avoid repeating the simpler *become proficient*.

Do It

Now that you have read about communicating in print, you'll become proficient at it only with experience under real world conditions. No one can learn how to write simply by reading about it. Only by "doing it"—writing many documents, relentlessly editing, and preparing draft after draft as required—will you develop a solid expertise in using writing to motivate people to accept your ideas and to do what you want them to do.

Do not be afraid to try, no matter how many mistakes you may make in the process. Every writer makes mistakes, and every proofreader misses mistakes. Despite the efforts of author, editor, and several proofreaders, this book no doubt contains a few passages that need correction or should be shortened.

But identifying our mistakes is how we learn, so the more you write, the more errors you'll make and eventually, the better you'll get at identifying and correcting them.

The same goes for writing with more words than necessary. The use of excess baggage may not be a mistake in the true sense, but it's a bad habit because it forces people to work harder than necessary to digest a message. To acquire the habit of being miserly in print, you must ruthlessly examine every word you use. Is each necessary? Are there shorter ways of making a point with the same or greater readability? Force yourself to cut and then to cut more.

Start with *widows*—words on a line by themselves. When you find a paragraph that ends with one to three words on the last line, find a way to eliminate that line. For example, "Our promotional program for June will consist of a series of magazine and newspaper advertisements on our new flavor adapter, coupled with radio and television commercials announcing our sponsorship of the concerts in Philadelphia and New York on the fourth and fifth of July" uses 5 lines. The last line could be eliminated by using narrower margins, but even with the same margins, the paragraph can be cut to 4 lines with a little editing:

> Our June promotional program consists of magazine and newspaper advertisements on our new flavor adapter, coupled with radio and television commercials on our sponsorship of band concerts in Philadelphia and New York on July fourth and fifth.

Work at it, and you'll find that what you write in a first draft is a gold mine of experience for eliminating excess baggage. There's no point in removing so much that your message loses meaning or is not vivid, and there's no point in being so fanatical that you write draft after draft just to eliminate half a dozen words. If you try to cut, however, you will cut, and you'll learn to focus on eliminating excess baggage only as a means to the end of improving your ability to transfer your thoughts to someone else.

That's what experience in writing is all about—developing the habit of communicating ideas rather than just stating them.

BIBLIOGRAPHY

Grammar and Writing Style

A Manual of Style. Chicago: The University of Chicago Press, 1982.

Hopper, Vincent F.; Gale, Cedric; Foote, Ronald C.; and Griffith, Benjamin. *Essentials of English.* Woodbury, N.Y.: Barron's Educational Series, 1982.

Montgomery, Michael, and Stratton, John. *The Writer's Hotline Handbook.* New York: New American Library, 1981.

Strunk, William, Jr., and White, E. B. *The Elements of Style.* New York: Macmillan Publishing Co., Inc., 1979.

Temple, Michael. *A Pocket Guide to Correct English.* Woodbury, N.Y.: Barron's Educational Series, Inc., 1982.

Editing

Ross-Larson, Bruce. *Edit Yourself.* New York: W. W. Norton & Company, Inc., 1982.

Job Application Letters

Hochheiser, Robert M. *Throw Away Your Resume.* Woodbury, N.Y.: Barron's Educational Series, 1982.

Word References

Boatner, Maxine Tull; Gates, John Edward; and Makkai, Adam. *A Dictionary of American Idioms.* Woodbury, N.Y.: Barron's Educational Series, Inc., 1975.

Chapman, Robert L. *Roget's International Thesaurus.* New York: Thomas Y. Crowell Company, 1979.

Lewis, Norman. *The New Roget's Thesaurus in Dictionary Form.* New York: G. P. Putnam's Sons, 1978.

Webster's Ninth New Collegiate Dictionary. Springfield, Mass.: Merriam-Webster Inc., 1983.

INDEX